PAUL BRUN

A Personal V

The royalties from this book are being donated to
the Paul Brunton Philosophic Foundation.

PAUL BRUNTON:
A Personal View

by

Kenneth Thurston Hurst

Published for the
PAUL BRUNTON PHILOSOPHIC FOUNDATION
by Larson Publications

International Standard Book Number (paper) 0–943914–49–3
Library of Congress Catalog Number: 89–45545

Manufactured in the United States of America

Published for the
Paul Brunton Philosophic Foundation
by Larson Publications
4936 Route 414
Burdett, New York 14818

93 92 91 90 89

10 9 8 7 6 5 4 3 2 1

The works of Paul Brunton:

A Search in Secret India
The Secret Path
A Search in Secret Egypt
A Message from Arunachala
A Hermit in the Himalayas
The Quest of the Overself
The Inner Reality
(also titled *Discover Yourself*)
Indian Philosophy and Modern Culture
The Hidden Teaching Beyond Yoga
The Wisdom of the Overself
The Spiritual Crisis of Man

Published posthumously:

Essays on the Quest

The Notebooks of Paul Brunton

(continued next page)

"To PB—now and always with heartfelt
thanks for a thousand memories."

"With filial joy I offer you this flower of days, that whatever fragrance it may have, shall tell of the days I spent at your side. And I know if I know you at all, that I can do no greater deed in return than to speak to my fellows of the unforgettably beautiful stream into which you turned my little boat, broken and halting though the words of stammering lips must be."

—PB

Though written by PB, and published in *Reflections on My Life and Writings*, no other words could so perfectly express my own heart as this book enters the world.

—KTH

"Remember always the spiritual teaching which I have tried to impart to you, as also the indissoluble character of the inner tie between us."

—PB to the author, January 20, 1944

To PB

The Guru

He came into my room and sat
Among my sacred things awhile,
There was great blessing in his eyes
And benediction in his smile.

Few words we spoke, yet much was said,
And after he had gone I knew
That in this quiet room I'd met
One of the Few.

—Hesper LeGallienne Hutchinson
West Redding, Connecticut
December 20th 1953

CONTENTS

Acknowledgments

Warmest thanks to four wonderful ladies, Gail Birnbaum, Carol DeSarno, Pamela Drix and Karey Solomon, who so cheerfully and willingly gave hours of professional transcription to put the manuscript in shape . . . to Anne Kandt Kilgore for her expertise in laying out and designing the photo section format and cover . . . to David Lewis for rendering first aid to the word processors . . . and to Jeanne Astor and June Fritchman for painstakingly proofreading the typescript. Sincere thanks also to those Wisdom's Goldenrod members who provided their recollections of meetings with PB for Chapter 23 thereby adding a further dimension to round out this portrait of my father. Finally my deep appreciation to all his readers around the world who have written me to tell what an important part my father played in their lives. Together, all of us, we share our memory of him—a memory that will never fade.

KTH

PAUL BRUNTON:
A Personal View

INTRODUCTION

My father, Paul Brunton, was a very private person. Hence I abstained for several years from the idea of writing his biography. But during the years following his transition in July 1981, so many readers of his books inquired about one that I began to reconsider. As the Finnish translator of his works, Mr Voitto Viro wrote me, "An outer and inner history of the man is always in a near connection with his message, which can be understood much better because these two are always reflecting each other."

Yes, so true. And there are hundreds, possibly thousands, of individuals today who could testify that their own experiences of Paul Brunton the person—and of themselves while with him—were more meaningful than thousands of pages of reading in spiritual books . . . that their personal contact with this unassuming man had an impact on them more profound than any other before or since.

The "biography" of such a man is in many respects an impossible task—certainly an impossible task for any single book. PB himself was usually reticent to discuss biographical details, and he recorded only a small percentage of them in his writings. Many of the most significant meetings and events of his life involved people who have long since left this earth without leaving any reliable record for posterity. Further, given the rarity of the inner state that made my father so special to so many, an entry he wrote in his personal note-books (see page 192 of Volume 8 in *The Notebooks of Paul Brunton*) is especially significant:

> My biographer will arrive with the cremator and attempt to portray my soul which, unfortunately for him, will already have fled. He will write about incidents in my external life, no doubt, and analyse my works with his dissecting knife, but my soul will be beyond him.

Certainly, I must agree, beyond the reach of analytical words on paper . . . though perhaps not entirely beyond the spirit behind the words of those of us who knew at least some part of him well and acknowledge the value of Mr Viro's excellent point. Further, as many friends said to me, "Sooner or later someone is going to write PB's biography—and they'll probably make a mess of it. You are the only person who has known him long enough and intimately enough to be able to do it. You knew him as a person, as a friend and as your spiritual guru for more than fifty years. You are the only living person to be acquainted with most of the details of his life. It is your duty to compile an accurate account of his life for posterity."

As the arguments mounted in favor of attempting such an account, I eventually began to feel an inner compulsion to undertake this task. The crowning factor was my awakening one night to see a young man sitting at my bedside writing intensively, concentrating on his work to the exclusion of all else. As I looked over his shoulder, I realized that he was *myself!*

I had already planned to write a short book outlining how anyone could use basic mental principles in everyday life. Most of these I had learned from my father. PB opened my eyes to the power of mind, to the fact that thoughts are things, and that we live in a mental world. In 1979 he said to me, "Why don't you consider writing a book giving a businessman's view of these ideas?" I demurred but the seed was sown. I found myself led into situations where I was asked to give lectures and workshops on the power of thought.

My ideas crystallized and I was able to condense them into a book *Live Life First Class!* published in 1985. This experience stimulated the creative juices and cleared the way for me to tackle the present work.

Yet so much of my father's inner and outer life remains unknown even to me that I cannot present this account as a "biography" in any strict or comprehensive sense. What I can hope to do is to convey something of the essence of this beloved and remarkably complex man while sharing many facts, anecdotes, and privileged points of view available from no one else. I can perhaps set a tone with which to approach understanding him as a man—focusing on events and memories that contributed toward or expressed his development and realization rather than cluttering the narrative with a multitude of chronological dates irrelevant to the real PB. I can share reminiscences that show his inspiring influence on me and on others whom I know, while keeping private any personal details my conscience tells me are for my knowledge alone. And I will minimize repetition of information already published, especially that available in his early books and in *Reflections on My Life and Writings*, Volume 8 in *The Notebooks of Paul Brunton*.

So many people ask me what sort of person was PB, what was he like, how was he as a father—they want to know about the private PB, the man behind the public philosopher. I can understand that, it's natural curiosity. So that's how I developed the theme for this book—it's a personal view of a man who meant so much to so many, including myself.

For each of us who writes about PB must frankly admit that we say much about ourselves at the same time. Few people got to know *him* as they knew others, for so much of his service was dedicated to helping us discover ourselves; and to do that well, he had to choose among his many facets the one that would at that time be most helpful to our needs. Being his only child, however, and having spent so much time with him in a variety of contexts through fifty-eight years, it is only natural that I do know him better than others do; but as there is so much that even I do not know, it is in that spirit that I have subtitled this book: *A Personal View*.

* * * * *

My father once told me that what people term "spiritual illumination" is no more than reaching full maturity, no matter how grandiose a goal it may seem to most of us. That is why we are here, he said. "In many ways it is just a beginning."

Although many regarded him as such by the end of his lifetime, Paul Brunton was not born a fully blown saint. Nor did he descend to earth as an already perfected being whose sheer presence served as a vehicle for inspiring and strengthening the best elements of others. Rather he paid his dues in the arena of life like the rest of us. He labored on the lonely reaches of the spiritual quest and underwent the same trials and tribulations as we do.

He once said to me: "I can tell you—I must be double your age!—that it's a worthwhile quest . . . and I've been at it since my teens. I've gone through the periods of scepticism, of foolish but complete faith that was misplaced, and all the other attitudes that the intellect, all that the emotions can pull you into. And I've come out of them and found my way to something that is there, that I know is there, something that is very real and that does not deprive me of my practicality or common sense. And yet, it is very, very far away from this world. It is there for me and it's very real, but it doesn't seem to me anything more than something that is there as much as this table. The ability to recognize this seems perfectly natural to me, and the peace of mind it has given seems quite natural to me. And what measure of truth I've found also seems natural—that's what is; that's how it ought to be. There's nothing dramatic about it."

But the key point is that my father came up through the ranks and earned his wings, no shortcuts, no free lunches. And therefore he sets the rest of us strugglers a wonderfully inspiring example—for if he could do it, so can we! Therein lies the exciting good news. All too often we tend to feel the grand goal is too far off, an impossible dream, something to be conjured with in the far distant future. Yet here is a man who has reached the goal, a human being just like us, who has committed the same kind of what we term "sins," made the same errors, fallen by the wayside several times, picked himself up each time—and at last achieved the final goal. For I firmly believe that my father reached the highest degree of spiritual development possible on this plane. Many others feel the same way.

This, then, is what I can tell of the man himself.

Kenneth Thurston Hurst
Naples, Florida 1989

CHAPTER 1

The Illumination

No account of my father can be properly understood without reference to the event that made him such an important figure to many thousands of people. Here it is in his own words.

"No reading of a spiritual book, no hearing of a lecture by another person can of itself bring illumination to anyone. The latter happens so deeply inside his consciousness that nothing coming from outside can penetrate there. Books, sermons and counsel are however good in their own lesser place to improve character and thus prepare the way for illumination. Studies and moral efforts such as are usually associated with the Quest are also on the outside surface and unable to enter into the depth needed for illumination. Prayer and meditation on the contrary are direct paths which are capable of reaching the plane of illumination. When they fail, as they often do, this is because they are not intense enough or not deep enough or not sincere enough to leave the ego behind.

"Since so few are ready to deny the ego, and fewer still able to do so, it generally works out that only when all their props and supports are knocked away from under them by events outside their control will any of them abandon their dependence on their ego and their belief that man can completely control his own life. Then, in utter helplessness, they will cry out and then only illumination becomes possible. But the catastrophe which can bring this about may have to be a formidable one, formidable enough to make its sufferers feel their utter powerlessness and insignificance. Some people are stricken with fear for their future while others may even be filled with suicidal thoughts through the feeling that there is no way out of the problem.

"Even if they have the conventional religious faith, that will not be enough to help them because the anthropomorphic conception of God does not correspond with the actuality. Its falsity deceives them, its self-centeredness keeps them within the ego and limits their outlook. It is indeed a concession intended to pander to their egoism, while at the same time bringing that same egoism under some kind of control. Hence, they are really still depending on themselves for help even when they believe that they are depending on God. Nevertheless, this does not mean that the orthodox conception of the Deity as given out to the masses is without basis or value. For it is false only because it is childish, and childish only because it has been made comprehensible to the simplest understanding. And is not such a conception of God better than none at all?

"When the results of popular education began to show in their lives, atheism or agnosticism spread among millions of the European working class during the nineteenth and early twentieth centuries. They rejected all religious consolation as being nothing more than a vacuous dream, appealing only to immature minds. Yet, the orthodox conception of the Deity which these masses rejected is not so illogical as it seems. It is a symbol, holding more content beneath the surface for those able to penetrate it. It is indeed symbolic. The developed intelligence realized that it is not to be taken literally and understands its higher meaning. The spiritually illumined person also disregards its outer form and sees the truth it is striving to tell, the reality it is seeking to suggest. With his entry into the state of illumination not only does this concep-tion of his own racial or national faith become highly significant, but all religions from the most primitive to the most cultured become significant. This was why the part of me which was appearing on the world stage, found it difficult to bear hearing anyone criticizing any religion, whether it was Catholic, Protestant, Jewish, etc. This was because I saw that God, whom I loved most of all, actually dwelt behind all religions and therefore to attack him was to attack my Beloved. I saw that every kind of religion helped some kind of person or mentality so that all the different kinds of religion, even though they seemed to contradict each other or were impure in motive and sometimes unworthy in conduct, were originally inspired by Divine Purpose to meet the different needs of different stages of evolution of the human race.

"Only a man in a higher state of consciousness can really depend upon God; because without such illumination he depends upon his ego to the end. No matter how much he prays for help he first tries to work out his problems by his own management. In the illumined state, he completely depends upon God for everything. He no longer has any ambitions or desires. The desiring ego is dissolved. Only a grave inner crisis involving the crushing of the ego can bring on this God-conscious state. Very often this is not possible of achievement by ourselves so it has to be done by an outside force or by outside circumstances. It is seldom that a man's own voluntary power can shatter its ego shell. However, he can assist the process somewhat through a self-discipline, purification and trying to raise himself to a higher existence. But in the end he has to acknowledge the ego's limitations and turn to the Short Path or else circumstances or disasters must crush him. He is so much in the ego that he cannot see outside it and therefore cannot, unaided, destroy it. Ultimately, if he remains on the Long Path, unpleasant and humiliating experiences must finish this process. It is the dark night of the Soul, the shock of being driven out of his personal complacency. He cannot help himself and feels that no one in the world can help him either. In that darkness he is utterly and completely lost, and there is no place to turn for light or relief, no way out at all. He is forced to give up and cry out in desperation to the great Nothingness which surrounds him. He loses the faith that God is merciful for he seems so deserted and alone.

"When this experience happened to me, I felt dead and empty inside. I was suddenly faced with an entirely new problem which caused me intense mental anguish for about a day and a half. There seemed to be no way out from it. Desolation and emptiness covered my heart. Confusion and torment filled it. There seemed to be no one to whom I could turn for help or advice, and I could find no solution within myself and had no power to do anything within myself. It was impossible not to refrain from crying and giving away to tears as I sank deeper into this black state. I became oblivious of my physical surroundings, as I was so intensely wrapped up in my descending thoughts. I felt utterly lost within myself. All the people around me seemed like empty shells. I felt no affinity with them.

Suddenly, I realized that this was a crushing of the self by an unknown power beyond myself. It was then that I began fervently to pray, feeling forlorn, humbled, terrified and lost. I did not pray for any particular one thing but prayed only for help in a general sense. I lost the feeling of the passage of time. I felt severed from earthly reality and became dizzy at the thought that I had reached the end of my endurance. Then I swooned. The moments just before I fainted were filled with indescribable horror. But I soon awoke. A tiny flame of hope appeared in my heart. And then it grew and grew. My first thought was that God was answering my prayers. I began gradually to feel close to the people around me once more; closer than ever before. Some hours later reassurance gradually returned to me and I felt mature and newly born. Enlightenment seemed to come.

"Next a feeling of oneness with God followed. I seemed to know and understand much that I had never understood before. My ego was going and my happiness increased every moment. I felt that this newfound faith would guide me through every possible situation.

"Previously, I had been somewhat of a dreamer and impractical. A big change in my nature took place and I became better balanced and much more practical. Previously I had disliked certain duties, but now I welcomed them and was able to perform them efficiently and correctly. I felt that I was able to put that wisdom into action. In all conversations, decisions and actions I did not need to think out beforehand what I had to say or do but immediately and spontaneously uttered or did whatever came into my mind. It was always the right approach, the perfect approach to the matter in hand, however trivial it was. This gave a feeling of absolute certainty as the result of these utterances or accomplishment of these actions.

"All day long I felt that I was in communion with God so that I was either praying or talking to Him, and he was constantly with me as my beloved companion whose presence I felt strongly. At times I would become so immersed in this feeling that I thought I was God! I felt that the real me was invulnerable. No one could hurt it whatever they did to the outer person.

"The Divine Presence seemed to be very near. In fact, I knew that it was in my real essence. Whenever any difficulties or problems arose, I found that all I had to do to solve them was to say, 'Not my will but thy will be done.' With enough patience, they would invariably work out in the best way. During the illumination whenever I saw something wrong in any situation and thought that it ought to be put right, this magical result was instantly brought about. It happened in widely different cases, such as the lack of certain needed things: they came into my possession; and in discord between two persons, I was able to put love into their hearts and harmony was restored.

"The outer personality who was the actor on the stage would express a wish for something but would place it at the same time under the higher will and say that it wanted that thing only if it was the Divine Will. Nevertheless, it seemed to get what it had wished for. Yet, it was not attached to the thing and was ready to relinquish it if it were not permitted by the Divine Will. Although there was desire in the sense of legitimate need, it was not attached desire. It was always subordinated to the Higher Will, for my over-mastering desire was to keep in harmony and communion with God. Under this rule all the lesser desires had to take a secondary place. The same applied to my worldly requirements. They were always met. For instance, when an important journey became necessary, and I had not the money to pay for it yet, almost at the last minute the money came to me as a gift though I had never asked anyone for it. I felt intuitively that every need would be provided for. And it was. I inwardly felt and outwardly realized the truth of the sentence in the Psalm: 'The Lord is My Shepherd, I shall not want.'

"The ordinary person is too attached to his desires to be able to get what he really wants from God. But he can, by the force of his ego, his ambition, his will power or his concentration of thought or desire be in a position to get some part of these desires satisfied. The illumined person is detached from desires and, since he is free from ambition, by stating even once only what he outwardly needs—since inwardly he is fully satisfied having given up the world—God brings it to him. But this is correct only when he is actually experiencing illumination for only then does he and *can* he truly depend on God. His thought, wish, prayer or word attain the power to become realized, magically fulfilled because he has stepped aside and allowed the infinite power to act within him. Prayer is sincere and its answer becomes possible when it becomes deeply felt and as concentrated as meditation when it asks God to take us away from the ego or to do something to set us free from the false self.

"The word 'I' was pronounced in me; I saw it was the only reality, all else was illusion. 'I' was in every person there but they did not know it and clung to its counterfeit—body intellect and desire—which blocked their way to Spirit. 'I AM' is the foundation of truth and reality of the whole universe. I saw my body as a mere shell and all other people's bodies as shells. I felt like a bird, *free* of all desires, really detached from everything. I was not the body and felt so free of it that I knew I could not die; in the real 'I' I would always be able to live for it was God.

"Previously I had been in intermittent ill-health, but during the illumination I enjoyed perfect health and abounding vitality. I did not lose the awareness of the 'I' or the 'I AM.' Its presence pervaded every hour of the day and persisted even during sleep so that I was both asleep and not asleep. I found that four hours' sleep was quite sufficient. In fact, I never really slept at all, but remained partly awake, the real 'I' being conscious of the fact that my body was sleeping.

"Although I had descended deep into my being and experienced Timelessness, I was still able to live in my surface being and experience time. The two experiences went on side by side. Deep down within my heart I lived in a sort of everlasting NOW. I was perfectly content with it and did not look to any future for a greater happiness. Whether I was looking at a beautiful scene in Nature or hearing beautiful music or merely doing some prosaic task, my happiness remained unchanged. I lived completely, vividly and intensely in the present moment. There was no past and no future; they were both contained within it. This was not like the ordinary man's Now which is based on the passage of time. This had a timeless quality about it. It was an unmoving stillness and things, events, people, came into and flowed out of it. I realized that the passage of time was an illusion, that everything which was happening to the ego was not making any difference to the real self, which remained the same. Looking back upon the past years I still seemed to be in the same eternal Now which I had been in when I first experienced it. It is as if nothing has happened since then.

"What happened to my sense of time, happened also to my sense of place. For the first time in years I lost the intense longing to return to India, which had until then seemed my only spiritual home.

"In the Light there was no struggle or fear. Here Nature was working willingly with her God. In my heart rose the mighty strains of Handel's *Hallelujah* Chorus. 'Hallelujah! The Lord God Omnipotent Reigneth for Ever and Ever.' The Power of God surged through my being with such force I realized that within myself, at the centre of my being, God was *always* there, strong, great, loving, blissful. And when I looked around at my fellows I saw that there too, deep within everyone of them, He dwelt, serene and quietly. Only they were not aware, not awake to this Reality. Still there He reigned, 'for ever and ever.' I wanted to say to them, 'Have no fears, my brothers, for we are in God, we are God, and with him there is only peace, and power, and love. Be brave for it is your heritage one day to know Him, to be Free in your awareness of His presence, to be joyous and peaceful in His enfolding arms. You will be compensated for all your suffering. I can feel your pain and sorrow but listen to me, I tell you that within your very self is only joy and bliss. One day you shall all know this truth, that is the inescapable Law!'

"My relationships with people also underwent a great inner change. I felt independent of them, and no longer in compelling need of their affection or even presence. I felt detached even whilst still loving my known and unknown friends. What I gave was free from possessiveness and liberated from futile longings. It was purer, and not the chained kind of love that it is with so many people. Therefore, there was also no dependence upon anyone for happiness. Happiness has to come from the harmony within and however welcome the love for or from the other person is, its loss will not then reduce one's own happiness. Love is the expression of this harmony. The infinite being loves us infinitely. To the extent that we can attune ourselves to it we too shall express love in our own relationships. Yet this love is not commonly seen and therefore what is commonly called 'love' is only a distant and distorted echo of it.

"I felt that my love for them did not diminish but on the contrary it greatly increased. There seems to be a fear in some people that they will have to give up their personal affections if they take to the spiritual path. The Truth is that they will give out more real love if it comes through their higher self than if they do not. I *was* Love; there was no need to go out of my way to love anyone. Similarly, in illumination I found I *was* the basic condition of all the other virtues. There was no need to aspire to any specific one of them. So instead of seeking them one by one it is enough to seek illumination.

"All my experiences now began to fit into a pattern. All fear left me. The world was transfigured with light. A few hours later whilst in bed in a state between sleeping and waking, I became conscious of a vast cosmic experience where the whole universe seemed engaged in constant movement with a dynamic power as the agent behind it. I felt that the entire universe was a unified whole in which everything related to everything else, and that I, myself, was at one with it. I could see now that everything that had happened to me in former years was part of a tremendous plan and had to happen that way. There was purpose and meaning in it all. Even the words that I and others had uttered were part of this plan. Even their thoughts and feelings and acts were within it too. There is a perfect harmony and pattern underneath all the jigsaw puzzle of the world's surface. When the pieces of this puzzle are put into their correct positions this harmonious pattern stands revealed. The world and everyone in it is controlled by a vast universal Mind. Every act and word is within this Mind or Plan. Within this great pattern is the individual's free will but ultimately, even the free will is controlled by this great Mind. Both the persons who believe in free will completely and that there is nothing higher than man's will, as well as the others who believe the extreme opposite, that there is nothing but

God's will, and that they must remain passive in their existence incapable of doing anything to change their lives, both these are partly wrong and partly right. Neither is the theory that the two forces exist side by side correct. The right view is that one is inside the other, like two concentric circles, a smaller lying inside a larger one. It is not as if the Higher Power and our own personal will are jointly responsible for all that happens to everyone every day of their lives. The Higher Power's will is ultimately alone responsible.

"Whatever any person decides to do, his personal freedom of choice will always be within the cosmic plan. So vast is this Plan that it has room for every possible choice. In this sense free will does exist. Yet, 'Determinism' also exists, but the former is within the latter like a smaller circle within a larger one. Both Indian fatalist and Western individualist are expressions of God's plan, since the Universal Mind is using them as well as other types for Its outworking. Whether people are good or bad, religious or atheistic, thoughtful or ignorant, they are all just as they should be in the cosmic plan. Everyone is growing up spiritually and growing through his experiences, whether the latter are high or low. Inner growth is the Law.

"There are two levels from which to regard the concept of free will. From the level of the enlightened, every little circumstance is preordained; every little or large thing—such as a scrap of paper or a revolving planet—is in a place allotted to it. Even 'evil' is ultimately a part of the World-Mind Plan. Everything moves and acts according to the Creator's pattern.

"I felt no urge to teach others, or to preach and arouse them, or to tell them what I saw by enlightenment. I played the part of a Witness, and silently carried on with my ordinary life. In my enlightenment there was no desire to teach others or to awaken them. This was because I felt everything was right as it was, everything was fulfilling God's will, each person was at his proper place in evolution and could not be at any other one. Every person is in the place which properly belongs to him at this particular time, whether he likes or dislikes that place. By 'place' is meant not only the physical environment but also the human relationships which pertain to that environment and the mental conditions which are active within him. By 'time' is meant that every event seems to be pre-timed and could not happen before its proper hour as set by the will of God. Every creature, person, incident and event falls into the pattern at exactly its right place. He is at his natural level, and needs no interference from outsiders. I saw it take enormous periods of time for people to attain the ego-free state and they must grow into it little by little. What was the sense then of trying to lift anyone to the highest plane of teaching; the feat is impossible to him and he ends in confusion, insanity or frustration. It is dangerous to give such teaching to those unready for it, as it stops them making the step-by-step upward effort they need must make. This is why those who are enlightened remain silent—unless they have a special mission to 'speak' to help others. There are certain individuals like Buddha and Jesus who had such missions. These messengers know that people cannot yet free themselves from ego, yet their love or pity was so great that they gave whatever little peace and comfort could be absorbed.

"The Cosmic Vision revealed the true meaning of freedom and fate, and showed how illusory is the feeling of free choice which we possess. The *Bhagavad Gita*'s description of Arjuna's Cosmic Vision is a perfect description of the actual situation. The world is therein pictured as being whirled around on a wheel, with God as the driving force. Every human being is on that wheel, revolving through the series of innumerable embodiments. Whatever it chooses to do, it will still be whirled around with all the others. Its personal freedom will still be fitted into, and limited by, that supreme fact. I understood perfectly the *Bhagavad Gita*'s statement that God is the real doer of everything and we only actors in God's drama, that those destined to be slain on the battlefield are already dead, and those destined to slay them are already marked down as instruments to effect this purpose. I understood too, Muhammed's constant injunction to resign oneself to God's will. In recognizing that we are parts of the pattern of circumstances and in accepting it, we let go of the ego, thus fulfilling and finishing the divine Idea in us. But if the Oriental fatalists sit down to wait for something to happen, they will be forced, eventually, to get up and do something about it. But even their misconception is part of the scheme. However, for someone to appear among them and show up their error and arouse them—even this too is a further part of the Plan.

"The world pattern is preordained in the sense that it is written out like a stage play. The author of the play is God. Each of us has an allotted part. Each has to play that part. He has no free will to reject it or to play another part. This is because he is the result of all that went before, cannot help being what he is, and what he has to do on the stage follows logically from what he is. Each person seemed to be enacting his allotted role, and saying and doing what he was ordained. Even I seemed to be one of the actors outwardly, although I was inwardly aware of what was happening and therefore, also played the part of a spectator. I looked upon the ego as something really separate from myself, or as a kind of puppet which I was manipulating. All other people looked like puppets to me too, although I could see that they were not aware that their higher selves were manipulating them—whereas I was aware, and could understand the process and the purposes of what it was trying to do in my outerself.

"Everything has to happen the way it does. Every incident is preordained by the past as well as by the Plan. Even the freedom of will to choose is only apparent, for the actual choice is itself preordained. Even our weaknesses and faults are used to bring about the preordained happenings. There is nothing wrong, nothing evil, everything contributes to ultimate good. Even seeming wrongs will be turned to right in some vast chain reaction which affects many other people whom we never know.

"I was much impressed by this Causal Chain, the way our acts and words start ramifications in long lines affecting many persons we never know or hear of, and across the world. Out of evil comes good, and out of good comes evil, if the chain of effects could be traced far enough. Good intentions may lead to evil results. Human existence seems to be involved in a gigantic web. Each part contributes to the whole web and its ultimate ramifications stretch across the whole web. Not only do we affect those whose lives come in contact with our own, but also those whose lives seem too remote and unlinked with ours. There are unseen ties and filaments connecting man with Nature, man with destiny, and man with man. There was a strong feeling of being an intended part of the design of this immense, even endless, world system which is so incredibly complicated. All I had to do was to fulfil my existence as that little part and ignore or discard any personal feelings about it. By a single large comprehensive insight, all is now explained. I see human life, especially my own life, under this new light. Those who have been driven by scientific discovery to concede large parts of the pattern yet believe that it somehow arranges itself, and that no Higher Power or Mind has anything to do with it, must therefore believe that the appearance of this particular pattern is solely a matter of chance. Why then does it show qualities of instinct, reason, purpose and other qualities associated with mind?"

CHAPTER 2

PB's Youth

My first recollection of my father is when I was a baby in my crib. I looked forward to his return home each evening. I knew that he was part of our family unit, along with my mother, and I recognized his particular scent as I rubbed my chubby fingers over his stubby beard. He used to dangle his fob watch over my cradle for me to play with it.

At that time he and my mother had been married for two years and were living in a flat which was the upper half of a two-story house at 76 St Alban's Road in Parliament Hill Fields, a pleasant suburb of North London on the outskirts of Hampstead.

Actually, as my father was to tell me years later, he had not wanted a child. He felt that properly discharging parental duties would interfere with his spiritual researches and would sap time and energy necessary for them. However, one of his first gurus, an American painter living in London (about whom I shall relate more later) told my father, "No, you must have this child. It is meant to be. It is a karmic relationship."

Many people ask me about my father's family, his parents. Truth is, I know little about them. I do know that his mother died when he was young and that his father remarried. PB called his stepmother "Aunty." I recall being taken to visit them when I was about two years old and the main thing that stays in my memory was being told I could not receive my presents until I ate up all my meal! PB's father died soon after and I know that PB helped support Aunty for the rest of her life. She died in a London nursing home in 1966. My father also told me that he had a younger brother who had died as a baby.

I know little about my father's early life. He was born and raised in London, England. I know scarcely anything of his background, but the following I do know because he told me himself: he was always a sensitive boy, and at the age of sixteen he had a mystical experience which increased his sensitivities more. He describes this experience on page eight of *Reflections on My Life and Writings*, Volume 8 in the series *The Notebooks of Paul Brunton*.

He described it thusly:

> Before I reached the threshold of manhood and after six months of unwavering daily practice of meditation and eighteen months of burning aspiration for the Spiritual Self, I underwent a series of mystical ecstasies. During them I attained a kind of elementary consciousness of it.
>
> If anyone could imagine a consciousness which does not objectify anything but remains in its own native purity, a happiness beyond which it is impossible to go, and a self which is unvaryingly one and the same, he would have the correct idea of the Overself.
>
> There are not a few persons who have known infrequent occasions when their ordinary mentality seems to lapse, when their feeling for beauty and goodness seems to expand enormously, and when their worldly cynicism falls away into abeyance for a short time. The place may seem perfect for this experience, but it may also seem quite the opposite—such as a noisy metropolitan street. There are many other persons who have known the beauty of a great musical symphony and felt its power to draw the emotions into a vortex of delight or grandeur. Such persons can more easily imagine what this rapturous emotional mystical ex-

perience is like. But they may not know that under the ordinary human consciousness there is a hidden region whence these aesthetic feelings are drawn.

It was certainly the most blissful time I had ever had until then. I saw how transient and how shallow was earthly pleasure by comparison with the real happiness to be found in this deeper Self. Before my illumination the solitary scenes of Nature's grandeur usually served as my greatest form of inspiration. I could become so absorbed in admiring such beauty that I would feel swallowed up in it for a period of time and fall into a tranquil state. After my illumination I no longer became totally absorbed in such scenes. They remained something separate from me: I was detached from them. The emotional exaltation they aroused was less or lower than the peace and joy I felt in the Overself. Yet this spatial detachment did not prevent me from enjoying nature, art, and music to an even greater and more satisfying extent than previously. The detachment gave me freedom, release from some personal limitations, and enabled me to feel and understand beauty in a larger and deeper way. I even became more attentive to detail.

The glamour and the freshness of those mystical ecstasies subsided within three or four weeks and vanished. But the awareness kindled by them remained for three years.

As a result he found himself out of tune with the harsh materialistic big-city vibrations surrounding him. In fact, he told me, they became unbearable. Finally, he decided he could do something about it, that he did not have to put up with the situation, that he had a choice—and that choice was to leave this world by the only means he knew, that of committing suicide. So being a well organized young man he wrote in his diary: "Commit suicide a fortnight hence."

And he proceeded to put his affairs in order. The thought then struck him: what happens when I die? Where do I go? His curiosity aroused, he went to the large British Museum

Library and asked the reference librarian for books on death. She steered him to the shelves carrying books on spiritualism. He took home half a dozen and eagerly devoured them. He found the subject fascinating—so fascinating, in fact, that as he had not finished all the books when his two weeks were up he postponed his impending suicide and went back to the library for more books. And again he had to postpone his suicide while he read with much interest whatever books he could obtain on the subject. Finally, he decided to postpone his suicide indefinitely!

My father had a teenage friend, Michael Juste, who shared the same spiritual ideals. They also shared an apartment in Tavistock Square. Their friendship lasted more than twenty years until Juste, who was a poet, broke off the relationship because my father, in his first book *A Search in Secret India*, used a poem by someone else (in fact his first student, Hesper LeGallienne Hutchinson—about whom more later).

My father told me he regretted the break. In fact, he felt Juste was quite right and that he should have used one of Michael's poems, which he regarded highly. Juste has had two volumes of poetry published, both long out-of-print. They were *Shoot and Be Damned* and *Many Blessings* (which I have in my possession).

However, back at the start of World War I, Michael Juste was a fledgling poet. I only met him once on a visit to England in 1952 when my mother took me around to his Atlantis Bookshop on Museum Street. I was rather put off when he termed me another wealthy American (far from the truth, incidentally) but my father later explained when I complained to him that that was "just Michael's way . . . and you must learn to accept people as they are."

My father writes on page 220 of Volume 8 in his *Notebooks*:

When I think back to those days, I remember when Michael Juste shared an apartment with me on Tavistock

Square in a massive eighteenth-century late Georgian house with lofty ceilings and thick walls, where two or three years later Leonard and Virginia Woolf turned the rooms into a publishing office for "The Hogarth Press" and helped to foster the so-called Bloomsbury Tradition in English literary life, with its high rationality, fastidious stylistic prose and irreverent youthful and unconventional criticism. Juste wrote brief inspired verses. His first publication, a yellow-covered little booklet, aroused the London *Times* reviewer to enthusiastic appreciation. He had extraordinary genius for poetic creation connected with spiritual sources, but turned his head to other kinds of work. He published an occult periodical for a few years and I know that he opened a book shop near the British Museum.

At the time I was born, in 1923, Michael Juste and my father belonged to a small group of Bohemians who met regularly and were all interested in spiritual matters. Among them was a colorful character known as "Bud." He was the scion of an aristocratic family, had served with gallantry in the First World War, but was regarded by his relatives as a black sheep and was paid a retainer to keep away from his ancestral home. Bud was easily provoked to anger and possessed a vocabulary more suited to a military barracks than to a drawing room. For a while Bud came to live with my parents at their small flat. But his colorful language and indolent habits brought my mother to the point where she decided he had to go. Nevertheless, she was fond of Bud and told me many stories about him.

Despite his temper, Bud had a heart of gold. Later when he became a Buddhist monk and went to live in Burma, my mother continued to correspond with him.

In my thirties, after she related one such story about Bud to me, I became curious, asked for his Burmese address and exchanged a few letters with him. He replied most graciously

and in such a friendly fashion that I came to feel a warm
regard for him. This regard was to manifest itself in 1959, as I
will relate in detail in a later chapter.

Other members of the Bohemian group included Joseph
Bevine, who was born in France and had come to England as a
teenager. I was to meet Joseph in October 1981 under interesting circumstances. My father had passed on in July of that
year and among my duties as executor was the awarding of
several bequests to various individuals. The last name on this
list was that of Joseph but I had difficulty locating him without
any address. Finally I remembered my father had told me that
Joseph had been a Vedantist so I wrote to the Vedanta Society
of Great Britain and they put me in touch with him. I wrote
him and made an appointment to call upon my next visit to
London. I found a pleasant gentleman of eighty-five years,
confined to his home by ill health. His nephew made a cup of
tea for us while I inquired why he and my father had not been
in touch for many years. "Oh, we just went our separate
ways," was his reply. But I found it fascinating to talk to him
because he was the last survivor of that small Bohemian
group. He had known my mother, my stepfather, Bud, all of
them. He said he had met my father at meetings of the Theosophical Society in London. I was enthralled when he told
me that most of the people in their group had been together in
their previous lifetime during the French Revolution. He
claimed that my father was a Marquis who had helped Joseph
and Michael Juste to escape from a prison where they were
awaiting the guillotine! Be that as it may, I presented him with
the pair of gold cuff links my father wished him to have. He
was to die soon thereafter—the last link with the group.

My father had told me tales of how the group used to spend
weekends camping in the countryside, trying to get back to
nature, but being city born and bred their outings weren't
altogether successful. They had trouble erecting tents and if it
rained they returned to town! But they were all spiritual seekers. They all shared a deep love for books.

My father confided in me that following his early mystical experience he discovered that he possessed certain occult and clairvoyant powers. He did not give me details but I gathered that they included the ability for astral travel and that he was able to visit other realms during his sleep. He found these occult practices fascinating. Gradually they occupied much of his time. He found himself reveling in them. And then, he said, he received an inner message, a warning: he had to choose between the sensational and the true albeit less spectacular avenue of solid spiritual progress. If he chose to continue developing his occult powers he could perhaps become a renowned psychic, but it would be with the understanding that this path was not the true spiritual path. Thus he had to choose. He knew his decision would be a weighty one. And he agonized over it. The temptation to continue his occult practices was strong, but he knew he had to leave the occult and devote himself to the true spiritual path. He told me that once he had made this decision his occult powers left him and he was no longer able to indulge in them.

During this earlier period he had become a member of the Spiritualist Society of Great Britain. He had wanted to find out what happened after death—if there was life on the other side of the veil. It was during this time that his occult powers were most active. He told me of an incident that occurred during this time which demonstrated his occult powers. He discovered that a well-known public speaker was using black magic for immoral purposes. So my father attended the next public lecture by this person. As soon as the "magician" began to speak, PB concentrated his own force and thereby extinguished every light in the hall. When the lights were switched on again, PB this time concentrated with such force as to explode every light bulb!

However, my father put these practices behind him and thenceforth concentrated all his energies on the practice of meditation. He not only meditated three times daily but often would go away for a weekend into the country for retreat in constant meditation. In fact, he told me that when he returned to London after a lengthy retreat the vibrations of the busy metropolis overwhelmed him so that to bring himself back down to earth he would imbibe a few glasses of beer—not his normal practice!

My father wrote extensively about meditation, especially in his earlier books *A Search in Secret India* and *The Secret Path*, as well as the copious notes in Volume 4 of his posthumously published *Notebooks*. These latter examine meditation from every possible angle and provide a wealth of material on the subject. His own extensive experience of the difficulties involved in balancing the deeply introverting effects of meditation with the outer demands of modern living bears fruit throughout his many valuable lines of advice and guidance on this theme—which for many years was his specialty.

CHAPTER 3

Early Days Together

People often ask me what it was like to have a spiritually advanced person as a parent. Looking back I can only say that while I always knew he was my teacher, he was something more than that—he was a very Special Friend who had always been with me beyond this particular lifetime.

I did not particularly think of him as a parent—he just was! And he meant more to me than anyone else alive.

"But what was he like as a person?" people ask me. They are understandably curious. They want to know what kind of human being he was. That's natural. I can understand that. Behind every public figure's outer persona there lies the private individual. And perhaps I was the one person in his life who knew PB intimately over so many years. He knew he could relax with me. He could joke and caper, even play the fool, without my being "disillusioned." After all, the man who held me in his arms when I was his only child, who told me how much he loved me, could not suddenly become distant as I grew older. Nor did he. There was a unique bond between us.

As I grew up I saw little of my father. He and my mother divorced when I was three years old. My mother told him one day that she had fallen in love with the man who was to become my stepfather, Leonard Gill, and who was a member of the young Bohemian group to which my father belonged.

PB immediately agreed to give her a divorce so she could marry Leonard. Leonard Gill went from Vedanta into the Anthroposophical Society as a keen student of Rudolf Steiner. Indeed he became head of the Rudolf Steiner book center and publishing company at 54 Bloomsbury Street.

My early memories thereafter of my father are sporadic. He would come to our house from time to time to spend an evening and to discuss plans for my schooling. He and my stepfather would engage in long friendly discussions about metaphysics. I recall hearing about such interesting personages as the "Buddha," and even then such names evoked strange familiar sensations in me. One such evening my father and stepfather were holding a heated argument about the relative reality of matter: my stepfather thumping the dining table and exclaiming, "You can't say this doesn't exist!" and my father explaining that the table was nothing more than collected energy in the form of atoms and that nothing was quite what it seemed.

PB would often seize an opportunity to be alone with me for a few minutes by asking me to show him the bathroom. *"Ou est le lavabo?"* he asked me once in French to test my schooling in that language. When we were alone in the hallway he would kiss me and I can still remember the rasp of his mustache.

When I was seven he obtained permission from my mother to take me away on a holiday. We went to Selsea on the south coast. We stayed in a boarding house but our room boasted a gas ring and we dined royally on Heinz vegetarian canned beans warmed in the tin over the flame. To this day I still have a zest for this savory dish! What a wonderful holiday that was. I still can recapture our walking the streets together while my father talked to me about the other world, the spiritual world. But he also knew how to regale a little boy: he took me on the funfair toy cars and we bounced around bumping into all the other cars. And once splashing around in the water I turned to him and cried excitedly that I could swim! He seemed as pleased as I.

In those days he told me about my "guardian angel" whom he said was an American Indian. This was enough to enthrall the imagination of any young boy and I often thought about my American Indian angel. Many years later when I was grown up and reminded him about my American Indian, he said, "Oh, that was just a fairy tale because you were a little boy. Your real guardian angel is your own Higher Self as is everyone else's."

Sometimes he would take me out for the evening, usually to a cinema. We both enjoyed films. Our favorites were comedies. It was a great thrill for me to go out with him. He brought a breath, a glimpse, of another world with him—an exciting world as yet unknown to me.

When I reached the age of ten I was allowed to spend Saturdays with him. At that time, in 1933, he had just returned from India and was putting the finishing touches on his book *A Search in Secret India* which was destined to become an instant popular success.

I recall taking the Underground Railway across London to where my father lived at 91 Fitzjohns Avenue, Hampstead, a cultured suburb high on a hill overlooking London. I remember helping him sort out the photographs for *A Search in Secret India*. It was here too that I met his editor, Clifford Potter, of Rider & Co. (before it was acquired by Hutchinson Publishing Company). The three of us were out walking one day and Mr Potter asked my father whether I was interested in these subjects he wrote about. I was tremendously annoyed when my father replied, "Oh no, he has no interest!"

It was at this time that he began to teach me how to meditate. I found it easy to do so and accepted squatting cross-legged side by side with him as a matter of course. He taught me how to mentally affirm "I am going within . . . to peace . . . and joy." It seemed the most natural thing at the time, yet instinct kept me from mentioning it to my schoolboy friends. Thus I was able to continue this practice by myself and would retreat to my own room at home and meditate regularly. Today, thanks to Transcendental Meditation and other organizations, meditation has become respectable in the West. But back in the 1920s and 1930s it was still little known and little practiced in the Occident. Yet to the sensitive seeker the time spent in daily meditation not only balances the rest of the twenty-four hours but indeed makes them bearable. The going within, as the Quakers put it, is renewing our connection with That which created us. It is the God-connection and serves to recharge our batteries and renew our spirits.

At times my father would take me with him when he visited friends and readers; we would often have group meditations. I can still hear his resonant voice chanting *"Om mani padme hum."* During these years in the thirties my father made trips abroad—to Egypt, and again back to India—but invariably he returned to England and we resumed our weekend relationship. How delighted I was when he presented me with the pair of mountaineering trousers he had worn when he wrote *A Hermit in the Himalayas*!

And then in 1938 my father left England for his first visit to the United States. I was not to see him again for nine years. A world war would separate us, like so many others. Yet we were able to maintain a fairly regular correspondence throughout that time. I possess every letter my father ever wrote me—and I treasure them. They were full of good advice to a young man. Typical was this one written at the end of 1944. I carried the original buttoned in my uniform tunic. I publish it here because it reveals much about the writer himself.

Meanwhile the indispensable task is to win the present war. In that task you are having your own personal share and adventures. I am proud of you as being a modern Arjuna. Krishna, as ever, is your own higher self. Keep your inner shrine within the heart reserved for the Ideal. Worship there the Spirit that is birthless and deathless, indestructible and divine. Life in this world is like foam on the sea, it passes all too soon, but the moments given in adoration and obeisance to the Soul count for eternal gain. The most tremendous historic happenings on this earth are after all but pictures that pass through consciousness like a dream. Once you awaken to the Real, you see them for what they are. And then you will learn to live in its serenity, however stormy and agitated the pictures are themselves. It is the greatest good fortune to attain such serenity, to be lifted above passion and hatred, prejudice and fear, greed and discontent and yet to be able to attend effectively and thoroughly to one's worldly duties. You too can get to this state—you have had momentary glimpses of it already— and live in it permanently. Only, patience is called for. When we can meet again, I shall help you with the benefit of thirty years' experience in this quest and with the grace of what I have found after having had to endure the vicissitudes, ordeals, temptations and tests which mark the way. You can learn painlessly in a few weeks what I had to learn through years of suffering and blundering. However the fact remains that I have found my way to the Overself, that I daily enjoy its blessed presence, that I have passed from mere existence into significant living and that I know there is love at the very heart of the universe. And now I want you (as well as others) to share in the fruits of this discovery. I want you to feel even in the very heat of war's activity that your Guardian Angel is ever with you, that it is not farther away than your own inmost heart. Nurture this unshakable faith, for it is true. Make it the basis of all your conduct, try to ennoble and purify your character incessantly and turn every fall into the stepping stone for a further rise. The quest winds through ups and downs, so make despair a short-lived thing and hope an unkillable one. Success won't depend on your own personal endeavors alone, although they are indispensable; it is also a matter of grace. And this you can get by unremitting prayer, addressed to whatever higher power you believe in most, and by the compassion of your guru. The readiness to go down on your knees for a minute or two, to abase the ego's pride in such prayer, is extremely valuable. This is what Jesus meant by becoming "as a little child": humility, inspired childlikeness, not stupid childishness. I occasionally remember the happy times we had together in London years ago—our picnics down the river at Richmond, your helping me on Saturdays with the sorting out of my office papers, your lunches with me at the flats in Chelsea and Hampstead, the mystical initiation I gave you which was to bear fruit a few years later, and so on. Although the future cannot duplicate the past, I hope we shall eventually be able to enjoy longer periods of association in the future. We have both travelled very far in mind and in experience since those days. The important thing is to be travelling in the right direction, that is, towards the realization of true ideals.

With my peace and blessing,

Affectionately,
Paul

CHAPTER 4

Early Spiritual Guides

One of the early influences upon by father's life and an introduction for him to Buddhist thought was Allan Bennett (known as the Bhikku Ananda Metteya). Born in London in 1872, an analytical chemist by profession, Bennett became a Buddhist at the age of eighteen after reading Sir Edwin Arnold's masterpiece, *The Light of Asia*. He went to Ceylon in 1900, studied Pali, and within six months had mastered this ancient language sufficiently to converse fluently in it. He made many close friends among the Buddhists of Ceylon. Having decided to enter the Buddhist Order and wishing to be ordained in Burma he left for that country in 1901 and became a novice monk with the name of Ananda Metteya. In Rangoon he inaugurated the International Buddhist Society and edited its illustrated quarterly magazine *Buddhism*.

In 1908 on a visit to England he helped in launching the Buddhist Society of Great Britain. On his return to Burma his health which was always very poor began to fail rapidly. Gallstone trouble was added to his chronic asthma. He was operated on twice and on the urgent advice of his doctors he reluctantly decided to leave the Order where he had now attained the seniority of Elder. He returned to England just before World War I broke out. Despite ill health he helped reorganize the Buddhist Society and restart its journal *The*

Buddhist Review. He pursued his appointed work of introducing Buddhism to the West with enthusiastic vigor in pamphlets, journals, and lectures in a stimulating and graceful style.

My father spoke highly of Allan Bennett, who died in 1923, a month before I was born. But I remember hearing both my father and my stepfather speak of the Bhikku when I was a child—they both had studied under him. Two of his works were published in book form: *The Religion of Burma* published by the Theosophical Publishing House in Adyar, Madras in 1929 and *The Wisdom of the Aryas* published in 1923 in London by Kegan Paul, Trench, Trubner and in New York by E.P. Dutton. His writing style was clear and energetic, and his illustrations of deep truths were couched in simple illustrations. He espoused the cause of Buddhism with vigor and presented it to the West both as a solution to the terrible dangers facing it and as a scientific explanation of the universe.

To the Buddhists of Burma themselves, he cautioned against blindly accepting their fate as Karma. Karma is not your ruler, he declared, it is your very selves: "You are the maker of your life and builder of your destiny!" A remarkable, determined personality.

My father writes of Allan Bennett on page 209 in Volume 8 of his *Notebooks*:

It was said of Allan Bennett: "His mind was pure, piercing, and profound beyond any other in my experience. His fame as a magician was immense." He carried a glass rod, potent with magical power. Bennett was tall, stooping, with raven black wild hair, a high broad forehead, and a pallor on his face. An expert in electricity and mathematics, Bennett was one of the most valuable lives of our generation.

PB also stated, as appears on page 222 of volume 10 in the *Notebooks*, titled *The Orient*:

It is my well-considered belief that Ananda Metteya was a Bodhisattva, come from a higher plane to penetrate those Western minds which could appreciate and benefit by Buddhism as meeting their intellectual and spiritual needs.

And let me quote from an article my father wrote for a journal called *The London Forum* in 1934:

> I was fortunate enough to become a close friend of the Bhikku Ananda Metteya, who was undoubtedly the first great authority on Buddhism to step out of the cloistered retreat of an Eastern monastery and to come to Western shores. He taught me something of the inner side of his faith; he initiated me into Buddhist methods of meditation; and he provided an unforgettable lesson in ethics by the beauty of his own personality. He lived the doctrine of love for all beings to its fullest extent; none was exempt from the sweep of his compassion.

I remember sitting with my father in a train in Switzerland a few years before his death and listening to him talk about Allan Bennett. "He was a most interesting and enlightened person," said PB. "Someone should write his biography." I thought to myself, well it won't be me as I don't know anything about him. And yet by synchronicity at the right moment, I discovered these two aforementioned books bound together in his own binding by my father and thus preserved for posterity. They have enabled me to pay public tribute to one of the early guiding forces upon my father. PB kept a photograph of Ananda Metteya on his living room wall to the end.

The next guide to play an important role in my father's spiritual life was the Indian to whom he refers in his first book *A Search in Secret India* in the chapter, "A Prelude to the Quest." Privately in conversation with me when recollecting those early days he would refer to this man as "the Rajah"—

for such indeed he was. In *A Search in Secret India,* my father describes meeting him in a small bookshop which specialized in recondite subjects.

> The speaker's face fascinates me. It is unusual; it would be distinguished looking among a hundred Indians. Power kept in reserve—this is my reading of his character. Piercing eyes, a strong jaw and a lofty forehead make up the catalogue of his features. His skin is darker than that of the average Hindu. He wears a magnificent turban, the front of which is adorned with a sparkling jewel; for the rest, his clothes are European and finely tailored withal.

The stranger invites my father to dinner, who then reports, "I received my invitation into the pleasures of curry, thus acquiring a taste which is never to leave me." (True! My father loved curried dishes; I remember well how he could prepare a delicious curry sauce to enliven the taste of everyday vegetables.)

My father continues:

> After that memorable evening I visit the Indian's home many times, drawn by the lure of his unusual knowledge as much as by the attractiveness of his exotic personality. He touches some coiled spring among my ambitions and releases into urgency the desire to fathom life's meaning. He stimulates me, less to satisfy intellectual curiosity than to win a worthwhile happiness.

The Rajah prophesied that my father would visit India one day and seek out the remarkable holy men whom they discussed.

> From that time I feel strongly that a momentous day will dawn which will find me at anchor in the sunny East. I reflect that if India has harbored such great men as the

Rishees in the past, and if as my friend believes, there may be a few of them still in existence, then the trouble of locating them might be balanced by the reward of learning something of their wisdom. Per adventure, I might then gain an understanding and content which life has so far denied me. Even if I fail in such a quest the journey will not be a vain one. For those queer men, the Yogis, with their magic, their mysterious practices and their strange mode of living, excite my curiosity and arouse my interest. The journalistic grindstone has sharpened to an abnormal keenness my concern with the unusual. I am fascinated with the prospect of exploring such little-known trails. I decide to carry out my fancy to its full proportions and when opportunity allows take the first boat to India.

My dark-skinned friend, who has thus clinched and rendered final this determination to trek towards the rising sun, continues to receive me at his house for several months. He assists me to take my bearings upon the swirling ocean of life, though he always refuses to act as a pilot across the uncharted waters which stretch ahead of me. To discover one's position, to be made aware of latent possibilities and to get one's vague ideas clarified is nevertheless of indubitable value to a young man. It is not amiss then if I pay my meed of gratitude to that early benefactor of mine. For a dark day comes when fate spins its wheel again and we part. Within a few years I hear seemingly by accident, of his death.

Time and circumstance are not ready for my journey. Ambition and desire lure a man into responsibilities from which it is not easy to extricate himself. I can do little more than resign myself to the life which hems me in, and watch and wait.

I never lose my faith in the Indian's prophecy.

The third and to my knowledge most important spiritual guide to my father in his early years was an American painter named Thurston living in London. My father said that he was one of the most remarkable men he ever met: "He was a phenomenally gifted clairvoyant and adept in the better sense who passed through the world quietly, unobserved but unforgettable by those he helped."

In Volume 8 of his *Notebooks* (*Reflections*) my father refers to Mr Thurston. On page nine he writes, "I then met an advanced mystic—an expatriate American living in Europe—who told me that I was near the point where I could advance to the next and higher degree of illumination."

Mr Thurston came into my father's bookshop in Lambs Clinton Way, Bloomsbury near the British Museum one day in 1922 and, like the Rajah, invited him to dinner. He remained an important factor in my father's life until his death in the mid-twenties. He authored at least two books of which I am aware although they are now out-of-print, copies of which my father gave me. *The Dayspring of Youth* was published in 1933 by Putnam's in London and New York. The author is identified only as "M" and indeed this is the way he was referred to by my father. The preface includes his thanks to MJ for having helped him edit the manuscript—this was Michael Juste, the boyhood friend of my father whom I mentioned earlier. The book itself is dedicated "To those who have served and have attained we dedicate this book as a memorial of brotherly love."

The Dayspring of Youth is not an easy book to follow. It attempts to explain the universal order of things from an occult viewpoint. Yet one paragraph from the introduction reads as though it could have been one of my father's books:

> Man is a prisoner within the atmosphere of this world, but his Higher Self awaits the time when he will release himself from bondage and return to it. This union can be accomplished if the student will but aspire and bring into activity those dormant properties of matter within him of which he has been unaware.

I treasure my autographed copy of this unusual work, as I do the few lines in M's handwriting.

Mr Thurston also anonymously translated and provided a new commentary to a classic occult book *Comte de Gabalis* by the Abbé N. de Montfaucon de Villars, published sometime in the 1920s by William Rider and Son in London. The first edition of this work was published in Paris in 1670 and its hero was cited by Lytton in his novel *Zanoni*. Alexander Pope refers to him in his dedication to the *The Rape of the Lock*. The Abbé de Villars himself lived from 1635 to 1673 and was an earnest worker for the cause of liberty and religious tolerance. According to M, "He awakened a desire for truth in the jaded though brilliant minds of that effete period and sought to turn them from the degradation of the times by pointing out the possibility of regeneration, doing much to elevate the thoughts of all who came under the sway of his gentle and persuasive influence." Like his other book, this one bears the imprint of "The Brothers" and the statement, "We seek to serve that thou mayest illumine thy torch at its source."

My father told me that during my mother's pregnancy Brother M contacted me before my birth by a clairvoyant trance and told my father that my spiritual name was "Jathaniel" (which means, he said, the Gift of the Lord) and that I would be spiritually developed. He said that I would be "farsighted, a commander of men." Thereupon my father looked up names and gave me the name of Kenneth, signifying a leader, an old Scottish name representing the Neth of the Ken (clan), the leader of the clan.

My mother also told me that Brother M had told her before my birth that he had had a vision of me sitting at a large desk as an adult, surrounded by books in the background, and that I would "have a lot of knowledge." In fact, I do indeed have a photograph of myself taken in my business office exactly as he describes.

PB wanted to show his respect for and indebtedness to Brother M by naming me after him: thus my middle name of

Thurston. In fact he reminded me when I was about thirty years old that Brother M had recommended that I employ the full name, Kenneth Thurston Hurst, as it would bring me good fortune. So although at school and in the Navy in England I had used the British style of K.T. Hurst, and had changed this to the American style of Kenneth T. Hurst upon coming to the USA, I promptly adopted the use of my full name. Perhaps it is a coincidence, but my professional publishing career took a marked upturn from that point.

Brother M specialized in painting lacquer and was employed by one of the largest department stores in London, which sent him all over the world to execute commissions for wealthy buyers. But according to my father, Brother M also traveled astrally and many times took him along.

Mr Thurston must have been a remarkable person, and I wish I knew more about him—I do not even know his first name. But I do possess a rare photograph of him which is included in this book.

He told my father, "I sometimes think of your future work as a giant statue, magnificent and beautiful to behold when it was made but now, alas, fallen into the sands, half buried, prostrate and crumbling. Your work is to disinter this statue from the sand and to raise it to an upright position."

These then were the three most important early influences upon my father's spiritual growth.

CHAPTER 5

Literary Influences,

Success Magazine

My father told me that there were three major influences upon his professional writing style. These were Arnold Bennett, Ralph Waldo Emerson and Elbert Hubbard.

Arnold Bennett was a prolific British novelist whose works sold widely and enjoyed popular acclaim although they had fallen off by the time of World War II. He wrote many interesting novels set in Midland towns in England. My father appreciated their craftsmanship and deftness of character and told me he had greatly enjoyed reading them as a young man. He lent me one of his favorite Bennett novels *Hotel Imperial* which tells of the inner workings of a large London hotel and the various personalities who staffed it. There are some spiritual allusions in the book; for instance, there is a scene where the hero attends a performance of *Der Rosenkavalier* at the Paris Opera House and the beautiful strains of the final trio lift him into a higher consciousness. I discovered that most of Bennett's novels had been reissued as Penguin paperbacks so I read them all. In fact, I took one of them to Switzerland on a visit to PB in 1977 and we read it together, discussing it as we went along during my two-week stay.

Ralph Waldo Emerson's influence upon my father was more in his subject matter than in his writing style, although PB admired his straightforward no-nonsense approach. He recommended when I was a teenager that I read the essay entitled "Self-Reliance."

My father often quoted the Boston Brahmin and spoke of him warmly. He regretted only that Emerson was not a vegetarian. It is interesting to note that Emerson used the term *Oversoul* to connote the ray of divinity within each human being and PB coined a similar word—*Overself*.

The third literary influence upon my father was Elbert Hubbard, known as the "Sage of Aurora, New York." Hubbard founded a cooperative printing and publishing company known as the Roycrofters. He published a magazine *The Philistine* in which he boldly expressed his forthright opinions. His upbeat positive style appealed to my father who was later to emulate it in his own magazine *Success*. Hubbard, who was to go down on the *Lusitania* during the First World War, was perhaps best known for his stirring essay, "A Message to Garcia." This was reprinted in the millions and used by governments and large corporations to inspire their employees. The Czarist Russian government bought rights to reprint it for each of their railroad employees! PB recommended it to me and I kept a copy in the top drawer of my desk throughout my business career to lend to my own subordinates as a help in encouraging them to develop their own initiative.

In the 1970s my father suggested that I publish a collection of epigrams by Elbert Hubbard; he felt that Hubbard's practical advice was timeless as well as entertaining. So after my publishing company made the necessary copyright and royalty arrangements with Hubbard's daughter we issued a handsomely designed and produced little book. Although it did not sell well, my father was pleased that we had done so and I was happy to join him in this tribute to a maverick soul.

Hubbard's style and pungent comments upon life set a benchmark for PB in the mid-1920s and he emulated both in the magazine he himself wrote and published called *Success*. There were only six issues of this magazine and I have four of them in my possession. Priced at sixpence per copy the magazine was literally a *tour de force* for one man: my father not only designed and published the magazine, and went out soliciting advertisements for it, but wrote most of the contents under various pen names!

It may surprise his readers to discover this side of his varied personality, but as a young man (he was thirty-one at the time) he believed strongly in positive thinking as enabling one to master the challenges of the business world. The magazines are full of his lively style of writing. In one of his editorials he states:

> The whole message of *Success* magazine can be briefly summed up in seven simple words:
> You Can Scale the Heights of Fortune!
> Oh yes, many things will be necessary—ambition, hard work, clear thinking, courage, ideals, persistent effort—much time must pass; the demons of self-doubt and discouragement must be exorcised; but—You Can!

He continues:

> If they can feel deep in their hearts that here is a thing they ought to do, but are too weak to do it, let them strengthen themselves with positive suggestion; let them utter that last affirmation:
> I am the Master of my fate; I am the Captain of my soul!
> And so reach to the untapped sources of Power which lie deep in the recesses of every man's soul.

This is indeed a little-known side of the man who was to write, starting a few years hence, his spiritually uplifting books. But my father believed and often told me that the same requisites for success in the business world are needed for achievement on the spiritual quest, namely, dedication, one-mindedness, determination, hard work, and inspired action.

A feature of the magazine was that my father sought out and interviewed business tycoons of the day—including

Frank Woolworth, Lord Leverhulme (founder of the mammoth Lever Brothers global enterprise), Sir Herbert Austin, Lord Trent, Sir Walter Runciman, and others. (Later he was to employ the same interview techniques in India, only then on holy men rather than commercial magnates.)

A sampling of the contents of the magazine reveals article headings such as "Make a New Start!" "Jobs in the British Colonies," "Promotion and How to Get It," "Turning Points in Ten Great Careers," "You—at Twenty-One!" "Are You Discouraged?" "Jobs and How They are Found," "There is More in You!" "Effective Speech for Salesmen," and so on. It was a dynamic miscellany of inspirational business writings which was to foreshadow the similar approaches of the Success Motivation Institute and the Dale Carnegie Institute.

There are echoes of Elbert Hubbard in all these magazines and it is now easy for me to see how my own style in business communications and in my own book *Live Life First Class!* (Mountainvue, 1988, distributed by Larson Publications, Burdett, NY) was greatly influenced, perhaps subconsciously, by PB's style at that time. I can now understand why he took an interest in my early business writings. Back in Dayton, Ohio, I used to write a monthly magazine for an advertising client and always included an upbeat inspirational editorial with a spiritual message; I used to send these to him and he would often make suggestions for improvement. For instance, he told me to omit the word "pretty" in a phrase "pretty good" as being slang and redundant. I found many years later, in going through his papers after his passing, that he had preserved all these writing efforts of mine: I was very touched.

Success magazine was published by Torus Publishing Company, with tiny offices at 7 Duke Street, Adelphi, London. Torus was the direct mail book service PB had founded following the bookshop which he ran with his friend, Michael Juste. My father confided in me that he and Michael had found it difficult to raise the enthusiasm to go into the bookshop on beautiful sunny days, and he felt he needed more time for creative pursuits. So he left the bookshop to Michael who developed it over the years into the Atlantis Book Shop, on Museum Street just off the British Museum.

Another feature of *Success* magazine was a section called "The Reading Lab" which carried book reviews. The reviews were all signed, most of them being by Raphael Hurst, my father. (Raphael was his given name at birth. He used this in signing many articles in *Success*, *Occult Review*, and other publications. "Ralph" was how my mother's family called him—like "Jack" for "John.") In reviewing one book my father makes a comment which foreshadows his *Notebooks* by some fifty years: "It is a slim volume and all the better for this because he has been compelled to state his facts in the smallest possible number of words—a procedure which is always of the greatest benefit to readers and one which compels an author to *think* as well as to write." In later years he would develop this style, and the last thirty years of his life were devoted mainly to writing brief paragraphs on a theme rather than expanding it into a narration.

A reader may well ask, "How could the philosopher Paul Brunton demean himself to write about commerce?" Let my father reply in his own words from the magazine:

> Money is the second greatest power in the world. Rightly used for constructive purposes, and backed up by the ideal of service, it can change the face of our society and remold human life, conferring innumerable blessings in addition to inevitably bringing benefit to the one who wields this power. Wrongly used for destructive purposes, irrespective of the rights of others, it can bring untold misery to millions as well as leading to the spiritual degeneration of its possessor. Such use, for instance, would be when a speculator corners wheat and sends the price soaring because he holds people at his mercy.

Furthermore:

It is not the aim of *Success* magazine to glorify the money spinner. The mere possession of wealth, self-made, is not the sole passport to these pages. The gilded ruffian who tramples on others is not a success in our view. Because we seek to portray in some of these pages such careers as have inspirational value for others, it will never be our purpose to bend the knee and worship Mammon. Character is to a man's career what the steel reinforcement is to concrete: without it all his works will one day perish into the dust.

Success magazine was an excellent idea. It performed a useful service and undoubtedly helped many young men get ahead but unfortunately the year of its publication was not conducive to any new venture being successful. For that year was 1929.

It seems fitting to end this chapter with an editorial from the July-August 1929 issue of *Success* magazine, because it discloses much about my father.

Success magazine believes in working really hard when you do work: it equally believes in thorough slackness when you are on holiday. Therefore it has taken the unusual step of combining the July and August numbers in the present issue. We know that it is not a convention to do this sort of thing, but then ours is not a conventional sort of magazine.

The next number to appear will be dated September. Because you have to wait somewhat longer for its arrival we intend to make it something worth waiting for. Some good things are in store for readers with valuable new features.

We, like our readers, are ambitious! Our purpose is to make this a journal which will render a service worth many times more than the mere sixpence that is paid for it. Help us to do so by giving your support, by introducing at least one new reader. Leave nothing to chance. Make sure you get this splendid September number and that you miss none of the subsequent regular monthly issues. And the only way to do this is to fill in either of the forms on the inside back cover.

The Editor

CHAPTER 6

His Literary Output

As a writer, my father was a true professional. He respected the power of the printed word and went to great lengths to sharpen his writing skills. They say that Horowitz still practices the piano for several hours daily even during his eighties; likewise my father never took his own craft for granted. He had a standing order with me to send him copies of any books my firm published on the art of writing. And indeed I would often buy and send him books published by other companies on writing. He believed that language is a living entity, not fossilized in a museum case but rather soaring and responsive to the expressions of new generations. He was opposed to anything which would impede the smooth flow of sentence construction. And he was alert to discerning trends in punctuation. For instance, he once pointed out to me how the hyphen has gradually lost its importance and is being used less and less. He believed that writers have a duty to be out in front of their readers and set the pace for more streamlined prose. For instance, when he wrote his book *The Wisdom of the Overself* in 1943, he persuaded his American publisher, E.P. Dutton & Co., to agree to his wish to omit commas between adjectives. The book thus duly appeared but the publisher said it created too much of a problem for the copy editors and typesetters who were not used to such avant garde formulation and regretted that they could not repeat the experiment.

My father learned his craft the hard way—as a journalist, always up against deadlines. His writing style was forceful, direct, and to the point. Indeed, as shown in the extracts from his *Success* magazine, it could be as pungent and exhortative as Elbert H. Hubbard himself. My father's early career encompassed bookselling (in person and by mail) and he had also been manager of Foyles, on Charing Cross Road, reputedly the largest bookstore in the world.

In 1931 he realized his long awaited desire to visit India and seek out its holy people. He returned two years later to pen his first book *A Search in Secret India* for which he adopted his pen name of Paul Brunton. Henceforth instead of being a journalist and reporter he would be an author writing on spiritual subjects. Therefore he believed a change of name was indicated, representing an important milestone in his own life and in his career. He actually chose the name *Brunton Paul*, which he felt was rather elegant, but the typesetter upon seeing the proofs jumped to the conclusion a mistake had been made and promptly changed it to *Paul Brunton*. My father accepted this change as a whim of the gods!

A Search in Secret India was his first book to be published and it proved an immense success, selling over a quarter of a million copies. In fact it was the bestselling of all his books. As he remarked to me once, after several other less "successful" titles appeared in print, "As my thoughts and teachings ascend into the philosophic realms, so my readership drops off!"

A Search in Secret India, however, was an instant success when published in 1934. It continues to be popular after many reprintings, and has been translated into several languages.

This is his story of a personal odyssey, his search for holy men and women in India to guide or inspire him on his quest. To this task he brought all his professional journalistic skills, coupled with an extensive background in spiritual research.

My father was a pathfinder. In this book he effectively helped introduce the terms "yoga" and "meditation" to the general public of the Western world. Interviewing yogis, fakirs and mystics, exploring a side of India previously unknown to most foreigners, he traveled the length and breadth of the subcontinent. His story became a tale of high spiritual adventure.

The London *Times* said of *A Search in Secret India*, "His work is excellent. It has life, colour, movement; readers will find their interest unflagging from the first page to the last."

Following the success of *A Search in Secret India*, my father determined to emulate it with a visit to Egypt and there seek out the unusual, the occult, and indeed, if it could be found, the spiritual. Shortly before he was ready to leave England to travel to Egypt he went down to his favorite county, Buckinghamshire, whose verdant countryside never failed to sooth and inspire him. (In fact, in a small Quaker village there he had written most of *Secret India*.) This time he had a vision. Ramana Maharshi, whom he would always refer to later as his beloved Master, appeared to him and told him that before he left "for the land of the waving palms" he should write a book of inspiration to share with his fellow men some of the spiritual uplift he himself had obtained. My father took this visitation to heart and promptly set to work to produce a short book which, as he told me afterwards, was the product of sheer inspiration. He wrote it quickly and the words flowed effortlessly from his pen. The result was the little book *The Secret Path*. This is still my favorite of all his books. The inspiration which lies behind it comes through the printed words. It is beautifully written and contains practical advice for everyday living on the spiritual path. Its slim size makes it convenient to carry anywhere and indeed I always take it with me on my travels.

PB once told me that the British Governor of Hong Kong told him that in December 1941, when the British were expecting to be invaded by the Japanese momentarily, the only thing which preserved his sanity amid the stress of that period was his copy of *The Secret Path* by his bedside.

When this book was selected by the Spiritual Frontiers Fellowship for their reading list, I was asked to write a study guide for it. This I gladly did and it has since been used by many study groups. I hope we will eventually have study guides for each of my father's books, including his *Notebooks*, as a service to readers who are living without the opportunity to discuss the books with others, or for use in small groups.

Thereafter my father journeyed to Egypt and wrote *A Search in Secret Egypt*.

As the reader will note, PB met fewer truly spiritual men in Egypt than he did in India; rather he met more fakirs and occultists. But the highlight of the trip was his spending a whole night alone in the Great Pyramid—the first European ever to do so.

My father told me that after having spent a night in the Great Pyramid, he was in a fever for three months, such were the after effects. But neither in that book nor in *The Secret Path*—where also he writes about the Great Pyramid and compares it to five other pyramids in the world, notably the ones in Central America, and notes that it was not a tomb as commonly supposed but a center for initiations into the ancient mysteries—does he explain the reason why he looked back and thereby broke the spell as he was being led to the secret chamber.

In 1987 at a conference I was attending in Chicago and during a session on the Great Pyramid wherein my father's book was mentioned, someone volunteered that the looking back signified the decision point where great souls were deciding whether to complete their transition or return to life on this plane, and of course those who relate their stories obviously made the choice to return. So it could have been with my father.

In fact he told me upon an earlier occasion that we make our decisions whether to reap the reward of our spiritual enlightenment by going to another planet or continuing to incarnate on this one to help humanity—and that we make this choice by our thoughts and feelings on the matter over a period of lifetimes. So it was that he elected to stay and help the rest of us make spiritual progress.

Interestingly enough in late 1986 an account appeared in the New York *Times* about the government of Egypt announcing that an archaeological survey stated that they were certain that there was a hidden chamber although so far they had been unable to locate it. This would have been the chamber my father was shown.

When he returned from Egypt, I once again had the privilege of helping my father sort out his photographs for the book and hearing firsthand of some his experiences.

The *Washington Post* said of *Secret Egypt*, "Amazing mystery, fascinatingly recounted. Books of this kind are rare indeed. This book will thrill you."

My father's next work was his least favorite. He wrote it on his second trip to India in 1937. And he wrote it quickly within a few weeks. He titled it *A Message From Arunachala* because it was written at the Ramanashram on the lower slopes of Arunachala. I have visited that very same cottage wherein he lived, a simple abode with open holes for windows barred to prevent animals from entering. Before the days of air-conditioning and indeed even without electricity, illuminated only by oil lanterns, that cottage must have been stifling under the harsh south Indian sun.

The book itself is a forerunner in style of his *Notebooks*. He used eleven categories (instead of twenty-eight as in *The Notebooks*) covering such subjects as politics, business, society, world crisis, religion, intellect, happiness, suffering, self and Overself. Under each heading he compiled paragraphs suited to the subject. As he writes at the beginning of the book:

> Try as I might I could not piece them smoothly together; they seemed but detached fragments; and time pressed too

heavily upon me to let me labor overlong upon the task of making them into a connected book.

Years later my father felt that *A Message From Arunachala* was far too negative in its outlook. He said it was too critical without balancing the picture properly and therefore he requested his publishers to let it go out of print. He took aim at modern society but later felt he had dipped his pen into too much acid.

For example, PB in this book describes the First World War in these terms:

> Mars hammered his piteous blows down on his victim, gloating over the blood and tears, and raised pyramids of skulls as monuments to the lack of good will among humans.

And yet the final chapter "Self and Overself" contains many inspiring passages. And the book ends with this beautiful paragraph:

> The hours passed unchimed and unrecorded. Face to face with the divine silence, I learnt the final message of Arunachala. It was the hopeful message of man's eternal, indestructible goodness. For at the very center of his being dwells God.

Having completed *A Message from Arunachala* my father forsook the sweltering plains of southern India and journeyed to the other limit of that vast subcontinent. He exchanged one small cottage for another. But this one was in the little-known state of Tehri amid the long snowclad range of mountains which separates India from Central Asia. He had hoped to travel to Tibet but could not obtain the necessary governmental permission. So he stayed nearby and for six months wrote daily in his journal a record of passing scenes and surrounding sights, of a few interviews and many meditations "in which I put my heart under a microscope and report what has come to me, what I have beheld in the shining hours of ecstasy."

My father describes the little robin which hops sedately around his bungalow as he sits outside writing in the sunshine, a robin who nests under the roof of his bungalow. As I read about his robin of some fifty years earlier, I watch my own robin from the deck of my cottage on Seneca Lake, the robin with whom I share territorial possession, and I think of my father's robin.

A Hermit in the Himalayas, the fruit of this period, is a fascinating book—most enjoyable to read. PB ranges over a panorama of subjects and treats them much more tolerantly and indeed more humorously than he did in *A Message From Arunachala*.

On page 80 of the American paperback edition of *The Hermit* my father uncharacteristically reveals his spiritual mission:

Some years ago whilst plunged in a yoga trance of profound meditation, I received a message, perhaps even a mission, but certainly a work to be done. This message came from four great Beings, angelic figures of an order particularly interested in the spiritual welfare of humanity in the mass, who have come close to this earth sphere from another planet. In obedience to this message, wherein I was bidden to become for a time a wanderer upon the face of the earth, I flit from place to place as the spirit moves me. I did not care then and I do not care now for public rewards. Fame and renown leave me quite cold and are therefore unwanted; money I require no more of than sufficient to live a decent existence among decent surroundings, and to meet the exigencies of the travels imposed upon me; pleasure I like to sample in small doses at odd intervals only. Although I accepted the task I refused its public side, preferring to let others do that part which was likely to bring them public rewards. It is more to my temperament to accomplish the fundamental basis of this task in quiet and secrecy. Literary work is but a side issue with me and as for reserves I have always the sense of divine providence backing me; I need no other.

In his foreword to this book Prince Mussooree Shum Shere of Nepal writes, "I am convinced that Brunton is one of the chosen instruments to reinterpret the half-lost wisdom of the East to those caught up in the mechanical life of the West, and thus serve His cause."

Few Europeans cared in those days to isolate themselves amid wild and rugged mountains far from the haunts of civilized society; my father was probably the only European living at that time in the state. His journal, *A Hermit in the Himalayas*, reads as vividly today as when it was written half a century ago.

In Chapter Six of *A Hermit in the Himalayas* my father writes about letters he receives from friends and readers. "My youngest student, a dozen years old in body but dozens of centuries old in soul, sends an affectionate note about his progress at school. He can do already, with ability and assurance, what many adults are still struggling to do—sit still and relax with thoughts successfully attuned to the Infinite." (page 63, American edition) When asked by a number of people whether he referred to Kenneth he replied in the affirmative and in fact he told me so himself.

Returning to England in 1936 my father decided to publish *A Hermit in the Himalayas* himself rather than offer it to his regular editor Clifford Potter at Rider & Co. So he formed Leonard and Company in partnership with my stepfather Leonard Gill. They rented a tiny office in Golden Square. My father dealt with the printer and my stepfather filled orders from the trade. The result was a disaster. My father had thought that the favorable response to his earlier books would carry over to this new one. But as he told me years later, "I soon realized that publishing is more than printing and ship-ping books . . . it's marketing, getting the books into the stores and creating a public demand for them . . . the publishing firms are geared up to do this, they know how and they have dozens of titles to support their efforts. I realize now you can't do it with just one book." So Leonard and Company folded, a painful financial loss, and my father returned to his regular publishers thereafter.

Indian Philosophy and Modern Culture was my father's doc-toral thesis. Any publisher will tell you that theses are notori-ously inviable for commercial publication and this book did nothing to shake that belief. PB was quite dissatisfied with it in later years, and, as with *A Message From Arunachala*, re-quested his publishers not to reprint it.

PB told me in 1960 when I broached the matter with him that he felt *Indian Philosophy and Modern Culture* was far too out of date in its comments on atomic physics and other scientific matters which have been quickly superseded by later de-velopments. So I took a copy and went though it to update it for the Sputnik era, and then submitted this to him. But he was not interested in having it republished. "Let it go," he said.

And so, the edition which I am looking at now with the notation in my handwriting at the front, "This copy marked up for revisions to be made for new revised edition 1960 NYC," is put back on the shelf.

His next book *The Quest of The Overself*, published in 1938, is a marked divergence from his earlier works. Whereas *Secret India* and *Secret Egypt* had been largely journalistic, and *Secret Path* and *Hermit* had been largely mystically inspired, *The Quest of the Overself* is the first of my father's books to represent the intellectual part that was to be so essential an element in his later work.

This book, particularly its latter part, especially the chapters on "The Overself" and "The Quest" should be required read-ing for all spiritual seekers. I cannot resist but to quote this last paragraph in Chapter 15 for it sums up what the quest is all about.

> Whoever faithfully follows this path will stand still at times with drawn breath when he perceives that a higher will than his own mysteriously intervenes in his affairs and always, in the highest sense, to his ultimate benefit. He will become an effective instrument in its divine hands. All events will become moves on a celestial chessboard. All things will conspire to work out for the best—bitter suffering no less than pleasant joys will provide accepted lessons in fortitude and wisdom. Even the harsh malice of his enemies will not be resented, for he will eventually learn life's last and loftiest secret—that every living creature bears the hidden tokens of divinity within its breast and is unconsciously striving amid its darkest sins for the deathless satisfaction, truth and power which exist in the Overself alone.

The Occult Review described *The Quest of the Overself* in these terms: "The authentic spiritual message, like a voice from far off, breathes throughout the whole book. Well worth waiting for."

That same year my father put together a book based upon private talks given to small audiences. It was published in England as *The Inner Reality* but in America under the title *Discover Yourself*.

My father felt this book was particularly suitable for readers reared in the orthodox Christian faith because it has chapters explaining the metaphysical meaning of much accepted Christian doctrine. In the chapter entitled "The Mystery of Jesus," for example, he writes:

> The coming of Jesus was a benediction to the world. He instructed and inspired men, he taught them the deepest secret of life and urged them to take to the divine path. He

exemplified in his own everyday existence a holiness that casts our common life in the shade.

As I look back into the past pictures of history and see his figure file past me, bearing the high dignity of the apostolic mark upon his brow, I receive renewed comfort and assurance. We are not left quite alone; God still sends companions for our stumbling feet, and apostles of the Infinite for our groping minds.

My father once told me that the true Crucifixion was not the nailing of Jesus' physical body to the cross, but rather the descent into matter of such a high and noble and advanced spirit: "It would be like you incarnating as a cat and trying to tell other cats about Mozart and Shakespeare when all they are interested in is eating and making love."

In his preface to *The Inner Reality* (*Discover Yourself*) my father revealed his own personal attitude toward his work.

I have found myself forced, little by little, along a path which I had never intended to tread, the path of writing sequels to my own works and explaining my own explanations. In short, I have unconsciously become more and more a tutor, and less and less a seeker. . . . I have freely given my time and life and learning to the cause of Truth, because I profoundly believe it to be the best of causes today. I know that its message is worthy of my pen, and its expression brings peace to my heart. . . . These pages were written because it was my duty to write them. . . . Utterly against my will and desire I have been forced to become, for all intents and purposes, a kind of detached tutor to the distant tutorless. Thus I retain my independence and they theirs.

A quirk of synchronistic fate came about in the year before my writing this biography. My cousin Karen Harms, living in London, reported to me that she had heard the actor Christopher Reeve announce on a radio program "Desert Island" that the book he would want with him if he were stranded on a desert island was *The Inner Reality*! He was then starring in a play on the London stage. I decided we should contact Mr Reeve and, to cut a long story short, he agreed to tape extracts from *The Inner Reality* (*Discover Yourself*) and *The Secret Path*. He came to our area and made the recording which has recently been released by Audio Literature of San Francisco.

In his preface to *The Inner Reality* PB continues:

> If in earlier books I was forced to accommodate the hidden doctrine of India to concrete intellect and popular experience, I now venture to pass upwards to a more exalted platform and make less of such accommodation. Indifferent as to whether or not it be palatable, I cast aside some reservations, some hesitations, and give the purer Truth as I know it. But the highest statement of this doctrine, scientifically covering the field of the universe itself, will appear only in my next book.

That next book was to be *The Hidden Teaching Beyond Yoga*.

The BBC Radio said of *The Hidden Teaching Beyond Yoga* that ". . . its extraordinary interest carries one without flagging through the whole of its 350 pages. The important turn given by Dr Brunton to the idealistic doctrine of the mental character of all experience is that the mental discipline in which he looks to engage us is related at every point to the act of living."

I find this book is especially significant for at least three reasons. First, PB there confesses that the first-person narrator of his earlier books was primarily a literary device—not accurately reflecting his own spiritual maturity at the time these books were written. Second, he there begins to unfold key elements of the philosophic position that characterizes the perspective of all his later writings. Third, it was the occasion of a personal experience of my own that bore fruit in later years.

My father had asked his publishers to send me a copy of *The Hidden Teaching Beyond Yoga* when it was first published in 1941. I read it through and found myself reading it aloud. Toward the end of this self-reading I experienced a vision of myself upon a public platform in the United States giving a lecture about my father and his philosophy—while in the wings my father was directing me from behind much as a ventriloquist juggles its puppet. I had at that time no plans for coming to America, and being of a shy and retiring nature could not imagine that I would ever be doing such some forty years later. But two years after my father's death I was invited by Spiritual Frontiers Fellowship to give a public talk about him in Philadelphia. One thing led to another and I found myself giving lectures about my father and his philosophy to groups across the country—even to Jungian societies in California—and some of these lectures are available on audio and video cassettes. So thus it came about—but that is by the by.

The second half of my father's magnum opus of the time was *The Wisdom of the Overself*, published in 1943. As my father later wrote: "In these two volumes there was an endeavor to bring together in a unity the elements of a scattered doctrine."

PB wrote in his preface to *The Wisdom of the Overself*:

> These two volumes now lay before readers a teaching which constitutes an endeavor to acquaint this epoch with the fundamental meaning of existence and which, in such explicit fullness, is for the first time written down in a Western language. An exposition in such an ultra-modern form was until now quite non-existent.

My father told me that when writing *The Wisdom of the Overself* it was as though an unseen Power guided his hand in organizing and arranging the paragraphs.

The Wisdom of the Overself not only contains fascinating chapters on dreams, sleep and death but also provides seven practical exercises which my father deemed indispensable for anyone seriously cultivating the spiritual life. Those who have practiced them over a period of years can testify to their effectiveness.

The Wisdom of the Overself received good press notices. The New York *Journal American* recommended it as "a book for those who wish to know the path to inner strength and, in fact, to a kind of godhood. Dr Brunton writes clearly and inspiringly. There is a World-Mind. In this book you get vivid glimpses of its potential operation right within yourself."

Certainly these two books represented the summit of my father's published philosophic thinking until that date. These were really meant to be one large volume expressing his exposition of the doctrine of mentalism, but because of pressure from his publisher and impatient readers, he published the first part as *The Hidden Teaching Beyond Yoga*. He was to regret this as the incomplete exposition stirred a controversy based upon a misunderstanding due to the work being split thus in two. In fact my father at his own expense had printed an Appendix to *The Hidden Teaching Beyond Yoga* which was later bound into subsequent printings in an effort to correct readers' misapprehensions.

My father's next book was not to be published for nine years—and indeed proved to be the final one published during his lifetime. He wrote *The Spiritual Crisis of Man* in 1951. It was poorly perceived.

In *Reflections*, Volume 8 of his *Notebooks*, PB wrote:

> *The Spiritual Crisis of Man* was indifferently received. It got neither attention nor circulation of any account. This was regrettable, for I had been allowed a peep behind the curtain of world events, behind the present pattern of the human scene on this planet, and there was real necessity for knowledge of it if all of us were not to go down into the gravest catastrophe.

and further . . .

Although I deny the criticism that *The Spiritual Crisis of Man* was a negative and pessimistic book, still some people thought that it was a dirge for a decaying civilization. They objected to being reminded of their grave peril and thereby made miserable.

Well, Jeremiahs are never popular and this book fell largely on deaf ears. It was the least popular of all my father's books. It warned of the consequences unless mankind were to change its present thinking and supplement its material drive with an equal if not greater amount of spirituality. It told us that we cannot build a better world until we have looked within, found the soul's light to guide us, and made certain inner changes.

And yet *The Spiritual Crisis of Man* also has its positive side. In many ways it was a trumpet call for the new age and it clearly points the way to a higher way of life. It contains many fine spiritual nuggets.

The New York *Herald Tribune* commented: "The book's written message is broad, its judgements frequently persuasive, its essential quality is one of warm humility."

Essays on the Quest, published posthumously in 1984, consists of fourteen essays found among my father's papers and put together for publication as a book.

It contains a beautiful chapter on the adventure of meditation; a far reaching explanation of karma in all its ramifications; a discussion on the mystery of evil. Chapters on Is the world an illusion? Is the soul in the heart? Cleansing of the emotions, Self-reliance or discipleship? make for worthwhile reading.

I cannot refrain from quoting from the chapter on "The Adventure of Meditation." It speaks for itself.

There is something in us of which we are not normally conscious. It is at only rare moments that we become aware—and that dimly—of a second self, as it were, of a nobler and serener self. We may have experienced such an uplift for only a few moments but we will be haunted forever afterwards by a sense of its tremendous importance. For we sense that we have then been in contact with something other than our ordinary self, sublimer than our ordinary self, yet despite that somehow related to it. Those of us who have passed through such an inspired mood, who have felt its serenity, tasted its power and obeyed its monitions know that only then have we been fully alive.

And then, of course, there is his voluminous *magnum opus*, published as *The Notebooks of Paul Brunton*, to be discussed separately in Chapter 27.

CHAPTER 7

Advice to a Young Aspirant

My father wrote me constantly during the World War II period when he was in India and I was completing my studies in England and later on active service with the Royal Navy.

If I now append extracts from several of his letters it is to highlight both his attitude to the war itself as a struggle between the powers of darkness and light and also to disclose his spiritual advice to a young man which contains sound precepts for any quester.

I have other files containing letters he wrote me in succeeding years up to his death in July 1981. But these tend to deal with personal and practical matters—and in any case they would fill a book by themselves. The letters here presented are in sequence and cover a period from January 1941 to October 1947.

January 22, 1941

I fully sympathize with the discontent and disillusionment that you express about modern social and political life. However it is no use to sink into despair about such matters but on the contrary equip yourself to rise up and play your part in service to mankind, thus helping the world instead of mourning over it. These matters are much more complex than you can understand at present for there are two sides to every question but you know well enough that at the bottom of all these troubles lies the ignorance of the spiritual purpose of life both on the part of the rich as well as on the part of the poor. Will it not therefore be a noble task to help remove this ignorance and thus indirectly help remove the material miseries which result from it? This is my aim and I hope it will be yours.

Well, I am sending you my inner peace and strength to help you in this terrible ordeal through which you are passing in England but it will always depend on your own mental receptive attitude how much of this you can take in. We must hold on and hope on knowing that the night is ever darkest just before dawn and we must try to equip ourselves to work for a better world for everyone when this nightmare has come to an end.

Peace and affection,
Paul

April 5, 1941

During such a dreadful period as the present there is little an individual can do outwardly. But amid all its horrors remember there is a Higher Power and that the contact with it is gained through making the mind still and calm; it is this distraction of attention inwardly which is the secret of yoga. In the very midst of these ordeals if you try to switch attention to this remembrance, you will, whilst remaining aware of the external happenings, simultaneously feel the inner presence of something that is like a Witness or Spectator of it all. That something is your divine self. I know this is hard to achieve at first but it yields to perseverance in a surprising way. And I am always here to help you. Thought, when keen and concentrated, conquers distance.

However I am sure you will come through this alright. We have something to live and work for. The same fate which separated us will also unite us at the proper time.

Love,
Paul

June 23, 1941

War is fought in the mind as well as with the body. This is where England has already conquered because our cause is right and just (despite our past errors) and the Germans suffer, I know, from a guilty conscience. The end I foresee for them is a nervous collapse, sudden and complete, when karma strikes the appropriate hour. There are many matters I would like to discuss with you relative to politics, economics and sociology, as viewed from an integral spiritual-practical viewpoint and with special reference to conditions after the war, as it is up to us who see a little deeper and farther to formulate policies for the guidance of mankind in this critical age. It is clear that the underdog will come into his own but this may be done crudely and brutally or wisely and peacefully. I am all for help to him but the harsh violent methods of the Communists stand convicted by their results in practice. In connection with this point please read the last chapter of my new book, *The Hidden Teaching Beyond Yoga*. Unfortunately the book does not deal much with "mystical" matters as it is intended to reach an intellectual-scientific type but the second volume which I shall write after the war, will reveal the higher mysticism which combines what is best in yoga, philosophy, science and action, whilst revealing that final truth which none of them can reveal.

I most particularly want you to get experience in handling correspondence of the best type, in shorthand-typing of letters and notes, so that later on you will be able to handle some of my letters on your own initiative and save me much time. As for editorial work you may also try to get into an editorial office, even in very junior capacity, so as to pick up the atmosphere and observe what goes on there. For later you will have to be Assistant Editor of two journals, among other jobs! Our plans for the journals progress well although they can't materialize until the war is over, but then they will start suddenly. Concerning correspondence again, you will profit more by study in American models as English letters are usually too stilted, formal and dull. Let Myron send you a couple of books on the subject. I want you to learn how to write a letter in an authoritative tone, lively and interesting, direct and crisp, to-the-point, and yet dignified enough to represent PB.

The passage in my letter of January last about wasting your time, ruining health, did not refer to taking a job—good heavens no!—but to your momentary and emotional statement last October that you were fed up with life and were going to become—of all things—a tramp! That all my high hopes of you should end up in a ne'er-do-well tramp was a shock to me as it was to you. But I am glad that your better sense soon reasserted itself and you dismissed the foolish notion. I had ambitions (!) in that direction myself when a boy and did actually materialize them for about three ghastly weeks when I decided that such a life was good neither to me nor to others and I dropped it like a hot cake. Life is too brief for such experiments, we have got lots to do to make something of our own lives and to be of service to mankind; the struggle is hard and bitter but we must not be cowards and run away from it. Perseverance along the RIGHT direction must end in success, not the kind which is measured merely by a financial-yardstick but the kind which touches the whole of man—mental, moral, physical and philosophical.

Love,
Paul

February 23, 1942

You must hold on bravely to your ideals meanwhile, knowing that the trials of wartime will come to an end eventually. Mankind is not only working out bad karma and being purified through present sufferings but also, if the anti-Axis forces win, preparing the way for a coming age which will be more spiritually minded and kinder to the poorer classes. I am quite confident we shall win and that Nazism will be exterminated. It is really a holy war against unseen evil forces using human instruments, like the one which preceded the destruction of Atlantis.

If you have not already done so I would like you to read H.P. Blavatsky's *Key to Theosophy*. It should prove easy, helpful, interesting at your present stage.

In your meditation start as if you are were switching on an electric current and aspire to the universal Mind, appealing to it to enter into your consciousness.

Remember: Courage, Calm, Confidence

With my Peace,
Paul

March 16, 1942

Here is an occult tip: Always use your full name when signing important documents or letters or even in general use. For your godfather "Thurston" was a great occultist himself. The old Egyptians believed in the magical value of names and the introduction of "Thurston" into your signature will bring good influence to you. Moreover the triple name is very impressive especially if you have ambitions to become a writer one day.

I am so happy that you often think of me. We must wait patiently until the German gangsters are smashed and the war is ended so that we may all meet again. Until then you know my love always enfolds you. Meanwhile fortify yourself with dogged faith in the Overself which is the only reality worth holding to.

Love,
Paul

April 16, 1942

If the leaders of the post-war world try to make it a better one for the toiling masses, then the war won't be all loss but will also be some profit. But our work is different; it will be to contribute those spiritual ideas which are needed to remove the materialism which is the real cause of all this wickedness which mars human history. Ever since you were a babe I have always hoped that you would join me in this work and it is beautiful indeed that you have come of your own accord and by your own inner and spontaneous growth to perceive its paramount necessity. To leave a corner of the world even a fraction better than you found it is to justify your existence as nothing else can. So it is with holy joy that I am waiting to welcome you when karma permits.

Peace and affection,
Paul

May 8, 1942

I was delighted to receive your latest photo. It shows quite an old-looking young man, full of growing wisdom, earnestness, self-control but perhaps a trifle too serious. Don't forget to laugh now and then, don't miss the comedy pictures at your cinema, develop a taste for good radio music, remember to present a smiling face to the world, for all this is a part of the philosophical life too.

I am very pleased that you realize now that pacifism and conscientious objection to war would be unworthy of you. They are ideals which are correct only for monks, hermits and those who have renounced the worldly life, but quite incorrect for you and I who remain in the world to serve mankind. And at a time like now when we are fighting such devils as the Nazi gangsters, who would destroy all spirituality, all truth and all religion, pacifism is sheer idiocy. The *Bhagavad Gita* explains that selfless action is much higher than self-centered renunciation. So we all have to support the war as a sacred duty but we can do it without hatred and simply to teach the Germans and Japanese that crime does not pay; if they learn this lesson we actually help them spiritually.

With my peace,
Paul

September 5, 1942

I am delighted that you read the book on Mahayana. It is an excellent and authoritative work. For your information it is well that you know that Mahayana doctrine is the nearest to our own. However it is split up into many sects and the pure truth is difficult to get hold of through books unless one has been personally initiated by a competent lama. I have had that good luck.

Love,
Paul

December 15, 1942

I shall be interested to hear after the war is over all about your adventures as a sailor and shall wait patiently until that happy time. Meanwhile amid all the dangers and hardships of your new life, your protective talisman should be your faith in the higher spiritual forces. You are fighting in a good cause, in a war which is a titanic struggle between the forces of good and the forces of evil. Remember the inspiring words of Krishna on the battlefield to Arjuna and do your karmic duty with confidence in the knowledge that you are doing what is right. You will be constantly in my thoughts and meditations.

With my peace,
Paul

January 14, 1943

Try to do your new duties with inner calmness and outer efficiency, but whatever you are doing, try to keep ever in the background of consciousness the remembrance of the Overself; it will be both a form of yoga and a protective influence. I never forget you and ardently work for the day when you will come into the blessed realization of the divine peace, joy, strength, understanding and unselfishness.

Love,
Paul

June 13, 1943

Although I have not heard from you since sending my airgraph last month, I feel impelled to send you a few more words because of the critical new phase the war is entering. So many years have passed since we last met and so much has developed in both of us that our next meeting will be an event indeed! And I am convinced that you are going to come through alright, so go ahead with faith in doing the duty to which war has called you. In my eyes it is a sacred duty because Nazism would stifle all spirituality in mankind and because Hitler is Anti-Christ.

If you have space to keep and time to read my new book, get a copy either from Myron (who has some of mine) or from Rider's (who have been instructed to let you have it if you write). The American edition will be much better, as type is larger and paper superior. By the time this reaches you, however, you may have read it and I shall value hearing your reactions to it quite frankly.

The divine arms enfold us all, despite all appearances to the contrary, and the divine love is always there. I want you to share this knowledge and this peace which I have found, so I keep you in my sunset meditations daily. One day we may do something together for mankind. I followed your suggestion and sent Mother something for her birthday. I am very much better in health again, although still needing rest. Once again, have faith fully. God will protect you. Wonderful powers are at work.

Love,
Paul

July 20, 1943

To find a few minutes for meditation every day is now becoming increasingly necessary for you, so that our inner communion may become stronger. The Divine presence is your best safeguard but you must look inside regularly to feel for it. 1944 will open a new vital period in world material and spiritual history.

My blessing and peace to you,

Paul

September 1, 1943

Any moments that you can snatch for quiet meditation will be valuable nowadays. Try to link up telepathically with me more clearly. The inner world of thought must be deepened to do this. Intense concentrated absorption for five minutes even will help. Yearn repeatedly for the consciousness of your true self, the divine soul in you. Such yearning brings its grace eventually in return. How happy you will be one day when you are established in its strength, light, bliss, serenity and insight! And how much good you will be able to do then! To find this inner soul is the real purpose of your life on earth. So stick to the Quest under all conditions, at all times.

My peace be with you, affectionately

Paul

January 20, 1944

Now that you are booked for active service, remember always the spiritual teaching which I have tried to impart to you as also the indissoluble character of the inner tie between us. Amidst all the dangers and hardships of wartime duty strive to keep open the inner channels of inspiration, protection and guidance with the divine power. It will be very hard to do so under the outer pressures but even two or three minutes' thought of it each day will be a help in this direction. I cannot overestimate the importance of simple recurring remembrance of (a) the Overself and (b) the guru, or trying to carry on in the atmosphere of such a remembrance. It is a yoga path of its own and is as good in its way as any other. But if you cannot do more, even mere recollection for a minute of the mental image of the guru will be a help. As for the bloodshed and horrors of fighting, well you will just have to steel your nerves and toughen your feelings by sheer effort of will power. Console yourself with the knowledge that it is only a temporary affair and will have to come to an end, when you can live the kind of life you want to. Life today is a terrible business and events underline Buddha's teaching about the ever presence of suffering and the consequent necessity of finding an inner refuge from it. Whatever happens try to keep your moral outlook undegraded by the outside pressures. Good character is the foundation for a worthwhile life, spiritually and materially.

With my cordial greetings for the festive season and peace and blessings for the coming year, Affectionately

Paul

March 9, 1944

I remember vividly the day you were born. There was much prayer and big things were expected of you. That is why you were named Kenneth which signifies "a commander." This letter will arrive somewhere around your twenty-first birthday. You have now attained manhood in the conventional sense. It is a suitable time not only to analyze the past for its practical and spiritual lessons but also to formulate ideals, ambitions, aspirations and plans for your life as whole. Such mental pictures, if constantly renewed and concentrated on, have creative power and help to influence physical conditions, and heartfelt silent prayer to your guardian angel for strength, wisdom and guidance will never be wasted.

Although I am unlikely to publish anything for some years I am still doing a lot of writing privately. Great revelations are coming to me and had I known twenty-five years ago what I know today much trouble and suffering could have been avoided, however I hope when we meet again I can pass something on to you so that you may profit by my errors and their consequences.

In the great strain and grave dangers of the coming months find your courage and serenity in the talismanic power of the thought of your higher self. It is always there.

With all my peace and love,
Paul

June 25, 1944

Amid the strain and danger of active service, keep the remembrance of your Guardian Angel, your divine Overself, ever in the background of your thoughts. Remember too the instruction given to Arjuna by Krishna on the battlefield: "I save them from death, whose minds are ever set on Me." (Chapter XII)

I send you my peace and blessing, affectionately,

Paul

June 1, 1945

The spiritual path is a call to renunciation of personal attachments, inwardly at least, and the animal nature. Both have to be overcome if inner peace is to be got. But once overcome, the world can be enjoyed without danger because your happiness no longer depends on it. If you let the natural desire for a mate be included in but transcended by the higher desire for spiritual realization, you stand a chance to get both. If you feel that the first is wholly indispensable to you, you may miss the chance to get either. I must tell you the truth, Kenny, that the Soul will not give itself to you unless you love It more than anything or anyone else. You have a great capacity for love in your nature. Properly directed by wisdom it will lead you to spiritual heights and human satisfactions. But directed by impulse, unchecked by reason, it could bring you into situations productive of much misery to yourself and others. Therefore I hope you will make it a part of your spiritual discipline to secure this balance and until you have secured it, to commit yourself to no decision without consulting an old man like me first! Much harm has been done to young aspirants by the pseudo-romantic nonsense and false suggestions put out by cinema, magazines and novels. "O son, though thou art young, be old in understanding. I do not bid thee not to play the youth, but be a youth self-controlled. Be watchful and not deceived by thy youth." I found these lines lately in a book called the *Quabus Nama*, written 800 years ago by a Persian prince, who was also a sage, for the benefit of his son. They are worth your study. Incidentally, as you are so fond of the *Rubaiyat* I ought to tell you that the key to its meaning is neither solely materialist nor solely mystic, but a combination of both. I have made an extensive study of Persian mysticism and discovered that the Persian character blends and includes the two.

Love,
Paul

September 6, 1945

Regarding the spiritual development, it will be easy for me to give you a further initiation when we meet, and thereafter you will make a quick advance in the consciousness of your higher self.

The goal, of course, is to become aware of it always but you have to become aware of it at odd moments first. With its presence made a living reality, you will understand why men like Jesus blessed humanity by pointing out the path. Everything else in life is uncertain and transitory, this is the only way to eternal Good and true Happiness. The lower self can be conquered but you will need grace for that—There is no peace until that conquest is made, you know that.

> My love and peace go out to you,
> Paul

November 25, 1945

If you haven't heard often from me recently it is because I am vainly trying to cope singlehanded with a six-man job. But your photograph is on my table and so you are not out of sight. I am glad you feel so strongly the urge to be with me again, after this trying separation, as it is not only derived from the ordinary human relationship between us but, what is more important in my eyes, the spiritual tie brought over from past births. I want you to spend a few years with me to receive training in spiritual advancement and worldly happiness. After that you can get on your own again, if you wish, but it will then be with material security provided for you and spiritual consciousness partially realized. And I want to do this partly because you are my chela and partly to fulfill my duty as a father, which I have hitherto never had the chance to do, owing to evil karma. Moreover there is my own practical need of a personal assistant to handle the practical side of living for me and also the confidential matters which can only be entrusted to someone of 100% loyalty. My order is to have a fully qualified secretary for the correspondence, as that is a full time job in itself, but you could also help out on typing notes and manuscripts.

That you have emerged from this terrible war safe and sound is itself a good augury for your future.

With all my peace and love,
Paul

October 31, 1947

You are mistaken in thinking that the guru places any obstacles or temptations in anyone's way. He does not have to do that. It is done by life itself, or rather by the peculiar karma arising out of the individual character and its special needs. The guru might note them and their existence and act accordingly, but he does not create them. In the end you yourself create your own temptations by your thinking, by your character, and by your karma.

As soon as you are ready for me, I shall be ready for you.

Peace be with you,
PB

CHAPTER 8

Arrival in New York

It was agreed that I would join my father in America after the war. But owing to his delayed arrival caused by shipwreck it was going to be many months before he could reach the USA. He had obtained a berth upon Norwegian cargo steamer *Taiwan* sailing from India after the war but on its voyage to England it collided with a freighter off Suez and my father, who had been sharing a cabin with a Bishop of the Church of England, had to be disembarked and remained in Egypt for four months. My father got away clad only in his pajamas and raincoat as he was sleeping at the time of the crash at 4:30 A.M. He was providentially saved from being drowned as his cabin was only a few feet away from the path of the colliding ship and it was flooded in a matter of minutes. He wrote me it was his personal karma which brought this about, that he had unfinished business in Egypt and that he had been meditating again in the Great Pyramid with "excellent results as happy as formerly they were eerie."

With his arrival date uncertain, I decided to remain in the Royal Navy for one more year rather than to accept demobilization in early 1946.

During this time my father reached America and went out to California where he enlisted two close friends, Paul Bernard Masson and Myron Daniel Frantz, to sponsor my entry into the US on a permanent visa basis. I completed the required forms and duly appeared at the American Embassy in London, where my naval uniform complete with combat medals certainly helped expedite my application. Thus when I finished my term in the navy on May 8, 1947, I already had my immigration visa in hand. It was then just a matter of securing ocean transport, but this proved more difficult as every ship sailing to the US was fully booked. I was competing with a multitude of GI brides! Nevertheless, I went around to all the shipping offices and put my name down in case a vacancy occurred.

I had hardly reached my mother's home that day when the telephone rang and I was informed there was one vacancy on the S.S. *Batory* sailing in a week's time. I accepted. My mother was none too pleased at my leaving so quickly after returning to civilian life, within a few days in fact. But I was anxious to rejoin my father and start my new life awaiting in the new world.

And so on May 16, 1947, I embarked, arriving in New York a week later. My father met my ship's arrival and after parking my suitcase in a safe deposit locker took me to lunch at a vegetarian restaurant I was to frequent often in the years to come. It was the Farm Food Restaurant on West 49th Street, between Sixth Avenue and Broadway. The restaurant featured entrées prepared from soybeans and nuts, and their imitation steaks and hearty soups were delicious. (I was indeed sorry when after forty years existence they closed in 1984 and the next occupant of the premises was a Japanese steak house!) That afternoon my father took me to a men's clothing store and bought me a lighter weight suit as my thick English tweed was not suited for the warmer American climate. (I was to return the favor many years later in Turin, Italy where I treated him to a new suit.)

Then he said, "Do you want to go home or would you like to stay in town and see a show tonight?" I plumped for the show and we went to see *Oklahoma* which was still running on Broadway.

My father enjoyed the theater and we saw many shows together in the years to come. I remember when the Royal D'Oyly Carte Company brought their Gilbert and Sullivan troupe to New York and I bought tickets for the series. The first performance was *Iolanthe* and at the conclusion my father said, "What a pity it's over, I'd like to see it all through again!" He enjoyed musical comedies and operettas, finding in them a delightful escape from his weightier responsibilities. Well do I remember when we saw *My Fair Lady* together. After the opening number "Wouldn't It Be Luverly" he leaned over to me and pointed out how its lively music and positive refrain put the whole audience in an upbeat receptive mood.

My father was equally fond of good motion pictures. Unlike a certain Oriental holy man who claimed he went to the theater merely to bestow his blessings on the audience, my father went mainly to enjoy the show. He had met several actors and actresses during his two visits to California. Charles Chaplin was a great favorite of his; in fact he dedicated a chapter to ruminating about Charlie and his art in *A Hermit in the Himalayas*.

I recall—one day in Auckland, New Zealand, in 1962—our checking the entertainment column of the local newspaper and my recommending we go to see a Charlton Heston film. My father was dubious but we went anyway and afterwards he said to me, "You were right, they wouldn't put Charlton Heston in a bad film."

He liked comedies—both the sophisticated Cary Grant and Katherine Hepburn genre as well as the Marx Brothers. Yet although he enjoyed going out to a movie he never had a television set in any of his homes. I pointed out that one could enjoy many movies, particularly some of the good old movies on TV, but when he was home he worked or read; and when he felt like relaxation he went out to dinner and a movie. Perhaps it was that in his home he built up certain vibrations of intellectualism and meditation and did not wish to have these disturbed by either television or a record player or hi-fi set. This was despite the fact that he loved classical music—indeed he refers in his books to the beauty of Beethoven's Fifth Symphony and his *Missa Solemnis*, as well as to works of Schubert, Mozart, Haydn, and Bach among others. In fact one evening, again in Auckland, we went to hear a small orchestra play Bach in a local church. We sat toward the rear and half-way during the performance my father leaned over to me and told me he could see a funnel of celestial beings pouring down over the orchestra and enjoying the music. He enjoyed opera and once we went to see the movie of *Tosca* together in Greenwich Village.

That evening in May 1947, after seeing *Oklahoma*, we took the New York Central train from Grand Central Station to Croton-on-Hudson where my father was staying in a small two-bedroom prefabricated home. It belonged to a friend of his, Mrs Joan Surbrug, who had a good position with Best and Company, the department store.

I might point out here that while my father adamantly refused to accept any gifts of money or other valuables from anyone, he would from time to time accept hospitality in the form of staying as someone's guest at their home *if* he knew them very well and respected them. So when Mrs Surbrug, who lived in an apartment in Manhattan, offered him the use of her new home for the summer months he accepted.

The house was situated at One Observatory Drive, a fifteen-minute walk from the railroad station. It was a pleasant suburban countrified neighborhood. (When my father and I went back again thirty years later out of sentiment, however, we found that the area had been so built up as to be hardly recognizable.) So here we spent the next six months. My father's writing desk was in the living room by a large picture window facing a copse of trees across the road. Two bedrooms and a small kitchen completed the premises.

I must confess that after six years in the navy I did not find it altogether easy settling down to a more disciplined existence as my father's acolyte. I had not seen him for more than eight years, and in that time I had grown from a young teenager to a young man in mid-twenties. At first, being a double Aries, I found it difficult to accept instructions from my father. Looking back, I feel that he was extraordinarily patient with me.

One day when he was out, for example, an insurance salesman came to the door and had no difficulty in selling me a disability policy. I paid the premium out of my limited funds. When my father came home he remonstrated with me and pointed out that it was not a wise expenditure on my part, especially in view of my limited funds. He was absolutely right of course, but in my egotistical arrogance I remember saying, "Oh, but you must let me make some decisions on my own!" Looking back it seems crass stupidity on my part; today I would welcome advice from anyone knowledgeable on such a matter.

Coupled with my own tendency to bridle was the aggravating factor of adverse force. As my father explained to me later there are negative entities, invisible for the most part, which inhabit this plane and are attracted to the light reflected by a spiritually advanced person. They cannot do any harm to that person directly so they seek ways to harm him indirectly and obstruct his work. Thus anyone who is not himself or herself advanced who lives in close proximity over a period of time with such a person becomes easy prey for these entities.

Etched clearly in my memory is the spectacle of my father emerging from the bathroom one morning while shaving, with half his face lathered, and he said to me, "Kenneth, I must warn you against the dangers of negative thinking."

"What on earth did he mean?" I wondered. I had never heard of negative thinking. Or positive thinking. He went on to explain that thoughts are things, and that when we emit them into the atmosphere they have to go somewhere. They have to be grounded, as it were. In my case, at that time, my negative thoughts were directed toward my father. He would be going out, for example, taking the train into New York City for the day, while I would be left behind to clean the house and cook the dinner, *etcetera*. I would start feeling sorry for myself. What a plum for the adverse forces! But negative thoughts aimed at a spiritually advanced person cannot hurt him. They are reflected back to the sender. As Gautama Buddha said, "If one does not accept a gift, to whom does the gift belong?" So my father was warning me that these negative thoughts would boomerang back to hurt me. This made a big impression on me. It was my first instruction from him after the war.

The lesson sank in. I mulled it over for several days and weeks. I realized that if that were true, then the obverse was true also; that positive thoughts, whether toward my father or anyone else, could only rebound to my own benefit. As a result, like the proverbial reformed drunk, I became a fanatic on the subject of positive thinking. And even to this day, some forty years later, I cannot countenance any semblance of negativism and always politely remove myself from the society of negative individuals as quickly as possible. Perhaps I swing to the other extreme but I do know that positivism has been a major factor in my success in business and in personal life. In fact I can't imagine life any other way.

One evening as he was leaving the house to go out, my father stopped by the front door, turned to me and said, "Thank you." Next day I asked him why he had thanked me; he replied, "Because you have started to restore your faith in me. When I thanked you last night it was because you had begun to restore your faith in me. I was grateful for your faith for it enabled me to pass you something. 'According to your faith, be it unto you.' Your eyes are going to be opened to things which will benefit you. Only the ego, the false self, stands in the way."

And so it was. Our relationship started to develop to a more mature level. But not before the adverse forces had one more fling—and a powerful one at that.

I awoke one night, clammy with perspiration, aware that some malignant creature was pinning me to the bed. I could hardly breathe and I was terrified. It so happened my father was out of town for a couple of nights; when he returned I told him about this frightening episode and he explained about the machinations of these psychic forces and their intent to harm him by means of me. He gave me a threefold technique to protect myself in case of any recurrence: first, to arise and put on all the lights in the house; then to take a shower; and, thirdly, to say outloud a mantram like "The Overself protects me" while visualizing a white light surrounding me as a protective barrier.

The attacks continued over a period of time but this technique proved extremely efficacious in warding off undesirable effects. Indeed, even some fifteen years later when I underwent a recurrence of similar psychic attacks, this same technique proved effective in affording full protection.

CHAPTER 9

The Summer of 1947

That summer of 1947 passed apace. We were still staying in Mrs Joan Surbrug's small home.

Mrs Surbrug was also a student of a Dr Frederic Levinson, a dentist empowered with much occult ability. Mrs Surbrug was acquainted with the famous Zen Master, Dr D.T. Suzuki, and she introduced my father to him. They got along very well together and one evening she took me to a meeting in Manhattan over which Dr Suzuki presided. I know that my father thought highly of this eminent Japanese gentleman and they met several times.

During this summer a student of my father's from Columbus, Ohio, Mrs Margaret Burkley, came to Croton-on-Hudson to assist with the secretarial work, typing letters for my father. She was a first-class proficient typist. We advertised in the local newspaper for a room to accommodate her. After we had duly selected one, I met her at the train station and escorted her to the nearby house where she would be staying. I left her to unpack and rest and was surprised a few hours later to receive a telephone call from her in a rather agitated state asking me to come and fetch her right away. I went down to the house and found the owner in an inebriated condition making advances to her! Fortunately in his advanced alcoholic state he presented no real threat and I was able to rescue Mrs Burkley and transfer her to a nearby hotel.

(Another example of adverse force manifesting itself!) It was also during this period that I met Ella May and Anthony Damiani—about whom more in a later chapter.

There were many visitors coming out to see my father. Some of them had read his books and written him care of his publishers to request an interview. He used his intuition to decide whether or not to grant one. He confided in me that when he read a reader's letter he could pick up their frame of mind at the time of writing—and thus was able to read between the lines, so to speak. My father would often end his letters to people with the statement:

"Peace be with you!"

He told me he meant this as an affirmation and that many recipients accepted it as such. In fact, he said many took it as the basis for a meditation and this enabled him to pass a spiritual force along to them.

The summer passed and I learned to serve in a secretarial capacity—typing and filing, and taking PB's dictation. Fortunately I had learned shorthand and typing at a Gregg evening school in London while I was waiting to go into the Royal Navy. These skills now served me in good stead. My father was a meticulous man and had carefully thought-out systems for office work. He studied each letter he received and gave due consideration to a reply. As the summer passed he often would give me the main points to be included in his answer and then let me compose the letter itself. Needless to say, being a double Aries, I much preferred the latter system!

It was at this time that I took to calling my father "PB." Until then I had called him "Paul." But everybody else called him "PB" and so I followed their example.

As the months went by I came closer to my father and came to understand him more. I learned to appreciate his infinite kindness. He went out of his way to avoid hurting any living thing—whether another human being or an animal or even an insect. He would cut the crusts off sliced bread and daily take them outside to feed the birds. His empathy for animals was remarkable. I remember once we were staying at some friends' home in Zollikerberg in Switzerland with their pet hamster left in our charge. The tiny creature normally was kept upstairs in the children's room, but my father pointed out that it would miss the children and therefore we should bring it downstairs with us. "After all, it has feelings too," he pointed out.

Later when he visited me in New York City he enjoyed playing with my cat, engaging its attention with a piece of string. "If I didn't travel so much, I think I would get a cat as a pet," he said, "but it's impossible for me to be able to take on the responsibility of looking after one."

It was during this summer of 1947 that I renewed my acquaintance with Myron. Let me introduce you. Myron Daniel Frantz was my father's first student in America. He was an attorney, specializing in corporation law, who resided in Chicago with his wife and two young sons. I asked him how he first became acquainted with my father. "Well," he said, "we had a summer cottage out in the country and on weekends we used to load up the car and go out there and I would always take an armful of books to read. This is how I first started reading PB's books. I was so enthralled by them that I wrote care of his American publisher, E.P. Dutton, and asked if it were possible for me to have an interview with him. I said that I would travel anywhere in the world for even a ten-minute meeting with him. Some months later, when I had given up hope of receiving a reply, a letter arrived from PB postmarked Los Angeles. He took me up on my offer and said that if I cared to go out to California he would grant me a ten-minute interview. I telegraphed back that I would be there the following weekend, and accordingly I flew out to the West Coast. I telephoned him upon arrival and he told me to come to his hotel at 11 A.M. next day. To my surprise and delight when the ten minutes was up he invited me to remain; in fact, he invited me to stay for lunch. And in the end I spent the entire weekend with him."

Myron became my father's lawyer and upon PB's departure from the United States his personal representative in America. He received my father's American mail, sorted it, forwarded it and sent form acknowledgments to the senders. All the time during the war years when my father was in India and until his return in 1947 Myron handled his affairs in the United States.

My first contact with Myron had been in 1940. My father asked him to correspond with me largely to dissuade me from my then avowed ambition of becoming a tramp and dropping out from the world. I was seventeen at the time. A warm correspondence developed. In December 1941 when America entered the war I wrote him "Dear Ally." Ally indeed he was and he became a warm and dear friend until his death twenty-five years later.

At the beginning of 1942 Myron volunteered his services to the US government and became a dollar-a-year man in Washington, DC. As the tides of war would have it my flying training in the Royal Navy Fleet Air Arm took place under the Royal Canadian Air Force and halfway through my course in Yarmouth, Nova Scotia, I was granted seven days' leave. I had written Myron about this upcoming furlough and with his characteristic generosity he not only invited me down to visit him but sent the money for the fare. It was quite a laborious journey necessitating train to Digby, Nova Scotia, ferry to St Johns, New Brunswick, and train to New York, where I arrived the following morning. My train came in at Grand Central Station and, having a few hours before my connection, I wandered around Manhattan and returned to Grand Central only to discover that my train south to Washington departed from Pennsylvania Station. In my ignorance I had not known there were two railroad stations in New York City. A taxi got me to Pennsylvania just in time to catch my train and Myron was duly waiting for me at Union Station in Washington, DC. He took me to his home in Chevy Chase, Maryland, where he lived with his wife and former secretary, Linda.

Next morning Myron and I took the bus downtown. I was in my heavy naval air cadet's uniform, more suited for England than the tropical humidity of Washington, so it was with relief that I adopted Myron's suggestion of doffing my outer jacket and traveling in my short sleeve shirt. I clearly remember sitting on the bus and asking Myron why was it that a genius like Einstein, who was in the newspapers that morning, was not a spiritual sage. He explained that one could be highly developed intellectually in one's sphere without necessarily being developed equally in spiritual directions.

My few days' leave went all too quickly but it served to cement a close relationship, second only to that with my father. So it was with pleasure that I greeted Myron when he suddenly appeared in New York that summer of 1947. I learned that his marriage had broken up and that his business affairs were none too healthy, in fact he had no practice and was really in New York City looking for employment. He took a furnished room in the nearby village of Ossining and developed the habit of telephoning in the afternoon and inviting me out for a cup of tea. PB had no objection and this became a regular habit. Myron was very helpful to me at this time, aiding me to make the adjustment from a life in the military to being an acolyte to my father. It was quite a change and there were many rough spots; however Myron proved a strong shoulder to cry on and gave me much good advice. Myron had an engaging warmth which endeared him to people instantly. He was a positive thinker par excellence, always optimistic, and indeed, like Mr Micawber, always on the verge of something turning up. But although he was extremely creative Myron had an uneven career and his talents were never fully recognized. He had good contacts in Washington and was close to Edward Stettinius when the latter was Secretary of State. There were no limitations to Myron's thinking and his plans were often grandiose. Later he became involved with the Greek shipping tycoon, Niarchos, and was instrumental in helping that magnate fashion his empire. But others took the credit for his best ideas so Myron never received the recognition he was due and was often hard up.

In 1949 he decided to follow the example of my father and change his name to signal a new cycle of his life: he dropped the Myron, and became known as M. Daniel Franz, and was addressed as Dan by his friends. My father thought highly of Dan and often commented on the latter's remarkable generosity. Years later in 1964 I received a telephone call from Dan to tell me he was entering the hospital for a lung cancer operation: he was calm yet prepared for the worst. The operation itself seemed successful but several months later his son Mike phoned me to say they had found Dan dead in his sleep in his small apartment in Los Angeles. When in turn I reported this to my father, he asked, "Did they say what his facial expression was like? That's important." Fortunately Mike and his wife Jane had commented on the fact that his face was lit up by a beatific smile. My father explained to me that this betokened a radiant transition and a quick ascent to heaven. My father went on to say that he felt that Dan was enjoying a period of bliss on the other side to compensate for the misfortunes and disappointments he had endured here. But that, for this account, remained in the future; in the summer of 1947 Dan was very much a part of our lives.

CHAPTER 10

Why PB Was a Vegetarian

My father was a vegetarian from his youth. I have been a vegetarian most of my life. At home I had never cared for the taste of meat as a boy and would only touch the well-done part of roast beef. When I left home I just naturally ate vegetables so it was easy for me to adhere to my father's strict vegetarian diet.

What were my father's views on meat eating? Why was he a vegetarian? Some of his views are given in *The Spiritual Crisis of Man* (1952: Samuel Weiser, York Beach, Maine 03910) and in his *Notebooks*, Volume 4, Part 2, *The Body* and Volume 5, *Emotions and Ethics* (1986: Larson Publications).

However he had, at various times given no fewer than six sound reasons. I repeat them here, in no particular order.

* *Cruelty.* My father was a sensitive person who would go to great lengths to avoid bringing pain to any individual or indeed any living creature. He would never voluntarily hurt anyone's feelings and in my own case would couch his reprimands carefully to avoid giving offense. He respected all forms of life.

The concept of deliberately breeding and killing animals for the sake of gorging on their flesh was incomprehensible to him—especially as he could not bear the thought of the brutal fashion in which these dumb animals were executed in the slaughterhouse. The thought of chickens being bred in artificially confined quarters, unable to move, and ending their brief tortured lives equally miserably, tortured his own sensitivities.

* *Repulsion.* The very idea of devouring a corpse repelled my father. To feast upon a dead animal's body revolted him; it was a barbaric concept which belonged to the animal world we are supposed to have left behind.

* *Health.* Today we are aware, even more than in my father's lifetime, of the chemicals and additives which are injected into animals bred for slaughter, many of them carcinogenic. My father believed in treating the body with respect and care, certainly never to deliberately poison it with such chemicals.

"But what about the need for protein?" is a question often asked. Well, the answer is simple; one does not need to eat meat to obtain sufficient protein. In fact protein is in most foods, including most vegetables. And regard the two strongest animals in the jungle: the gorilla and the elephant. Both vegetarians! The gorilla eats mostly bananas and the elephant is content with grass. Yet both are immensely strong. No weaklings they!

My friend Dr Arthur Broekhuysen tells me as this book is readied for publication that a recent German television program featured scientists unequivocally stating that a complete diet does not have to include meat in order to supply all the vitamins and minerals necessary for good health. Nothing is lacking from a vegetarian regimen.

* *The Effects.* It has been said that we are what we eat. In the fifteenth century lusty monarchs like Henry VIII gave full rein to their passions and cruelties—and we are all aware how they gnawed large chunks of meat as their staple diet. Eating animal flesh makes us more like those very same animals, because we absorb their vibrations and thereby lower our own

consciousness. Human life is enough of a struggle without taking on the characteristics of the animal world in addition.

* *Unnatural.* Carnivorous animals have long curved teeth to enable them to rip the flesh they are masticating. But human beings do *not.* Our teeth are not intended for meat-eating but rather for vegetation. Our teeth are shaped the same as those of animals which do not eat flesh. Nature never intended humans to eat meat, as shown by this reason among others.

* *Hatred and Criminality.* My father also believed that part, at least, of the criminal element in society is the direct result of souls incarnating into human shape while still carrying a hatred of humanity for the way they were treated when animals. The holocaust perpetrated upon defenseless creatures in the name of scientific research, the inhuman caging of helpless chicks and steers, creates its own karma as these forms of life unconsciously seek revenge. When will we learn?

CHAPTER 11

Arizona—1947–48

Ohio—1948–52

In September 1947 my father told me he was leaving to travel west across the United States and would be unable to take me with him. So I accepted the invitation of Myron Frantz to share a rented house in the neighboring town of Ossining with him and his son Larry, who had just graduated from college. I had to get a job quickly and with no skills or experience to offer an employer took a position as clerk in an import-export company in New York City. Fortunately the Gregg shorthand I had learned back in England enabled me to secure a quick promotion to stenographer.

Two months later a cable suddenly arrived from my father from Tucson, Arizona: "Give notice immediately and join me here." Though it was a test of faith, I handed in my notice to my employer the same day and a week later flew to Tucson. This trip necessitated an overnight stay in Chicago where I telephoned Myron's ex-wife Nancy and next morning was picked up at the hotel by her and her new husband. They gave me a tour of the windy city and drove me out to the airport for my flight.

Upon arrival in Tucson that night I was met by Bernard Masson. The name was not unfamiliar as he and Myron had been enlisted by my father to act as my sponsors for my permanent immigration visa to the United States. Bernard was a retired businessman. He and his French wife Ida lived in a trailer in the yard of the ranch-style building rented by my father for the winter.

"Rancho de las Palmeiros," as it was called, was twenty miles outside Tucson, which was a small somewhat sleepy town in those days. As he drove me out to the ranch, Bernard told me that he had studied my father's books and philosophy for many years and that he and his younger brother Jacques and his wife Diane had come from Los Angeles to spend the winter close to my father. Upon arrival at the ranch I found in my room a typed sheet outlining my duties and including this instruction from PB: "If you must indulge in the filthy habit of smoking kindly do so outside away from the building."

I greatly enjoyed that winter in the sunny desert. PB said the terrain reminded him of India and, as I was to discover years later, it was similar to the dry Deccan of the Punjab. My secretarial duties were not onerous and I had time to explore the surrounding countryside in company with the large watchdog which belonged to Bernard.

One afternoon Ida ran excitedly into the house exclaiming, "There is a rattlesnake in the garden!" We all went out and found a baby snake which PB asked me to remove and take outside the compound. Another test of faith! I was reminded of my father's own snake-handling experiences as recounted in his book *A Search in Secret Egypt*, particularly the following account:

Once, when I had slung a particularly thick and exceptionally large specimen of a snake around my neck for not more than a single minute, I had experienced a sudden slipping away of my mind from its earthly surroundings, and a bewildering psychic state supervened. I felt that I was losing my physical moorings and that the inner world of spirits was opening up. I seemed to depart from our whirling ball of land and water for some dark, ghostly, supramundane sphere whose atmosphere was definitely evil. I did not relish the idea of falling into such a condition and losing my "grip" on things with creeping death so close to my face; I let the snake fall gently to the ground. Immediately, my consciousness reverted to normal and was focused once more on the familiar physical world around me. This happened only once, but it was unforgettable.

Had I sensed the snake's own state of consciousness? Did it function in two worlds at the same time? And was one of them a nether world of horrors? Who can say?

However I had no such insight myself as I put the snake out in the shrub!

I was often invited to visit the home of Jacques and Diane. They were renting a newly-built villa on the outskirts of town. I liked them both. Jacques was an expert dealer in precious stones and traveled worldwide. He often regaled me with tales of his visits to the major capitals of the world, tales which ignited a desire to see them myself, a desire to be realized in years to come. Their young son Jeffrey was to grow up to become an eminent Indologist and would write a bestselling book on Freud which was the subject of a two-part article in the *New Yorker* magazine.

At the ranch Ida Masson prepared outstanding vegetarian meals. She always preceded dinner by playing Beethoven's Sixth ("Pastoral") Symphony twenty minutes or so beforehand: this conditioned me like Pavlov's dogs so that until this day I cannot hear that beautiful music without feeling hungry!

A succession of visitors came to the ranch. Among them, I was pleased to see, was Myron Frantz who stayed in Tucson for some weeks and visited the ranch daily to work with PB.

The dinner table discussions were always interesting. My father would invariably proffer some spiritual or philosophic topic and embark upon a lengthy discourse which held the rest of us spellbound. Yet often he would solicit others' views and treat them with the utmost consideration and gravity.

Dinner often proved a leisurely affair; my father regarded it as a relaxing occasion following the day's work. We would usually retire to bed afterwards.

Another visitor was Edward H. Spicer, an early student from back in England who had come to the States in 1940. He had owned a pharmaceutical company in the United Kingdom and had started another one in Pasadena, California. I had known Mr Spicer in London and can still recall how proud I felt when he had accepted as from an equal adult my statement as an eleven-year old schoolboy that the atmosphere in churches was kindled by the thoughts of the worshipers rather than any intrinsic spiritual vibration in the buildings themselves.

Ted Spicer was a keen Rotarian and indeed was responsible for my joining this organization some years later when I became a businessman. Some twenty years later while lining up for a taxi in the rain at Calcutta Airport I found myself sharing a cab with two Californian businessmen who were members of his Rotary Club and knew Ted well.

However this idyllic state of affairs was not to last. One day PB informed me that we would be leaving the ranch in April, 1948, and that he was planning to travel abroad. However to fulfill his parental duty toward me he had arranged for me to meet the owners of an advertising agency in Dayton, Ohio. He said he had had a vision in which he saw the president of this company taking me under his wing and training me in business matters. And that is exactly what happened. I went to Dayton for a weekend interview which resulted in being given a position with the agency as trainee. I spent five happy years learning from an outstandingly capable executive Herman Hutzler, and also had the good fortune to be groomed in character building by his wife Norma. So I really had the best of both worlds.

My father came to Dayton three times to visit me during my five-year stay there (in 1948, 1950 and 1952), and in 1949 I journeyed to Chicago to be with him for a week. He stayed at

the Lake Shore Drive Hotel, long since converted to con-
dominiums but then a prestigious hotel. And the ubiquitous
Myron Frantz was there at the same time; only now he had
changed his name to Daniel to signify an important new
period in his life. Here he was following the example of my
father who had changed his name from Raphael Hurst to Paul
Brunton when his first book *A Search in Secret India* was to be
published.

During his visits to Dayton my father would always check
up on my progress, both with myself and with my employer.
He would stay for a couple of days and then I would drive him
to Columbus, seventy-five miles to the north, where there
was a small group of readers with whom he met. Among
them was the Reverend Roy Burkhart, minister of the First
Community Church, who was an avant garde minister for his
day.

At the beginning of 1952 my father visited Dayton and
showed me the proofs of his forthcoming book *The Spiritual
Crisis of Man*. At that time the title was not definite and he
solicited my views. I remember suggesting *The Spiritual Crisis
of the World*.

CHAPTER 12

PB and My Mother

In July 1952 while still living in Dayton, Ohio, I decided to take my mother on a trip back to her homeland of Denmark. Born there, she had emigrated to England with her parents, brothers and sister before the First World War. She grew up in London and had met my father at a meeting of the Theosophical Society. PB married her, Karen Augusta Tottrup, in 1922. My mother was a very good woman, much given to charitable activities. She was also somewhat psychic.

When she died in August 1972, just six months after my stepfather's death, my father wrote me:

> There are two sides to death. There is the side which we who are left behind experience and we feel sorry for ourselves and miss the other person, but there is also the other side. A spiritually sensitive person, like your mother, is guaranteed a quick ascent to heaven.

At another time my father told me: "Of course your mother was spiritually sensitive—otherwise I could not have been attracted to her."

My mother's younger brother, Basil, once told me that on my parents' wedding day he had taken Ralph (as my father was then known) into a public house and bought him a whiskey to celebrate. When I later recounted this to my father he exclaimed, "Oh, not whiskey! Perhaps a beer, but nothing stronger, not even on my wedding day!"

Well, in that summer of 1952, it so happened that PB was also spending most of the year in Denmark. But he expressed interest in meeting up with my mother again, so I arranged it. We had lunch together in Copenhagen, and thereafter went for a walk through the old part of the city. I walked behind them so they could converse privately.

A few days later I visited my father on my own at the house were he was staying. It belonged to a Danish mystic named Martinus whom my father held in high regard.

My father returned to the United States early the following year, 1953, and I made arrangements to spend a week with him in New York in April of that year.

* * * * *

Many years later I told my father of my experience the night my mother died in August 1972: I awoke abruptly and fully. The time was exactly 1:30 A.M. Suddenly, I was aware of the presence of my mother. Impossible, I thought. She's 3000 miles away in England.

Just then I saw her standing by my bed. But something was different—for she was dressed in the "flapper" attire of the 1920s, with short skirt, close-fitting hat, and her face was youthful and unlined. She was smiling at me, a beautiful, radiant, loving smile. Her presence was overpowering, and I pinched myself to make sure I was awake. Gradually she faded away, and I was left staring into the darkness—wondering.

Next morning a telephone call from London announced that my mother had died at 7:30 A.M. local time: allowing for the six-hour time difference with New York, that was precisely the moment she had appeared to me.

But why had I seen her as a young woman? Then I knew! It was her way of telling me that she no longer suffered, that she was free from bodily pain, and that she was commencing a glorious ascent to heaven. The power of maternal love had triumphed over space and distance. And I knew that my mother was all right.

"Death, where is thy sting?"—it had none!

CHAPTER 13

Connecticut and Brooklyn: 1953–58

In the spring of 1953 I took a week's vacation to visit my father who was then staying in New York City. During this visit I came to the conclusion that I did not wish to spend the rest of my life in Dayton, Ohio, and that therefore it was necessary for me to leave. Upon returning to Dayton I therefore gave my notice to the advertising agency for which I worked—somewhat reluctantly because I would be leaving behind the known for the unknown. So it came to pass that in July of 1953, four days after obtaining my U.S. citizenship in the fourth federal district court, I packed my few belongings into my Studebaker and drove east.

My father had rented a cottage for that summer in Brookfield, Connecticut, and I succeeded in renting a room in nearby Danbury. So I was able to drive to Brookfield and help him with his office work every day. Brookfield was a pleasant country spot, and indeed my father writes of it in *Reflections*, Volume 8 in his *Notebooks*:

> When I lived in that little Connecticut cottage, the water I used for making the cups of jasmine tea which warmed me in the early mornings and slaked my thirst in the mid-afternoons, came from a spring close by. It had a neighbour, a brook that leaped after rains from stone to stone but sometimes dried up completely. The spring itself never

went dry, never stopped giving its beneficent draught. My happiness was just like that spring. It bubbled all the time, unfailingly fresh.

Those idyllic days that summer we worked in the mornings and then spent some afternoons touring the countryside. My father enjoyed visiting the small local libraries and browsing among their book and magazine collections. We meandered through country lanes and back roads leafily dappled with shade and sunshine. PB said that the attractive landscape of the state of Connecticut reminded him of his favorite county Buckinghamshire back in England. There he had spent much time when he was able to escape from London, and indeed it was there, as mentioned, that he wrote his second book *The Secret Path*.

Each weekend I joined my father in a brief thirty-six or forty-eight hour fast. He had introduced me to fasting during our time together on the ranch in Arizona back in 1947. At first the idea had seemed horrific to me: not eating for a whole day or two!

Back in Arizona, he had given me some notes to type which explained the physical and mental benefits of fasting. (These notes were preserved and have been published in his *Notebooks*, Volume 4, Part 2, *The Body*.) Six years later now, the idea did not seem so strange to me. We would usually break the fast by going to the local supermarket for bread and jam which we would consume with gusto at my two-room apartment in Danbury in the late afternoon. "Yes, fasting does give one an appetite!" said my father. I greatly enjoyed these times shared together. Our relationship had passed from the awkward discipline of Croton and Arizona to an easy intimate sharing.

But the summer passed. In October PB announced he was moving into New York City for the winter. I followed and took a small apartment in Brooklyn and embarked upon a six-month job hunt. Although I learned many lessons from this experience the frustration of not being even a tadpole in the New York advertising market after having been a large fish in a small pond in Dayton depressed me. I saw my father regularly and one day complained to him that I could take it no more: "I'm going to walk down 42nd street and continue right into the river," I blurted out.

"Oh, don't be so silly!" he said. But then he proceeded to teach me an invaluable lesson. "Visualize strongly and affirm that the right job for you exists, the job which will afford you work satisfaction and gratification as well as a good recompense; know that this position exists, the right job for *you*, and it is only a matter of making contact with it. So visualize it daily coming closer and closer to you, coming into your life and circumstances."

I followed my father's advice and soon was rewarded by exactly the right job for me: in fact, if I had succeeded in obtaining any of the other jobs for which I had been applying they would not have led me to the ideal publishing career which was to follow.

"Success in business is an equation of ability plus opportunity," my father stated. "If you have the first then you must be patient and wait for the second." Both lessons were to stand me in good stead throughout the rest of my life. Such was the practical application of my father's philosophy. And indeed I learned much from him that could be used in everyday life.

One day my father and I were walking along a street in New York City when he observed a poorly dressed man sitting on a stoop. "He looks as though he could use a dollar," said my father. "Why don't you give him one?" Which of course I did. So I learned not to respond indiscriminately to beggars but to look for those in genuine need.

My father was staying at the old Holly Hotel in Washington Square, which now has long since been taken over by New York University and converted into dormitories. It was then a pleasant area and I often met him for lunch and strolled with him around the neighborhood.

At this time I lived in Manhattan Beach, Brooklyn, in a four-room apartment on the third floor of a residential building.

134 / *Paul Brunton: A Personal View*

An added advantage was that I had an attic with ample storage space. So my father left his trunks and suitcases and storage cartons with me while he traveled. During the five years I lived there, my father often came over and we spent several hours looking for items in this low-ceilinged attic. In the summer it was quite stifling under the narrow roof and many a time, disheveled and sweating, I reminded myself that this had to be some kind of test as we rummaged around!

Sometimes my father would stay overnight with me in Brooklyn and we would travel into Manhattan together by subway the next morning. The journey took about an hour and my father commented that it was a waste of time for people to have to travel so far to their occupations. I remember one morning our being joined on the train by a young woman we knew, Mrs ML, who asked PB one of the most sensible questions I have ever heard any spiritual seeker pose.

"How exactly do we get started on the quest?" she asked. "What do we have to do?"

My father replied: "First, by acknowledging the existence of a Higher Power that lends purpose to our lives. Second, by practicing the remembrance of that Higher Power throughout the day, by going within and taking a Godbreak. Third, by setting aside time daily to try to commune with that Higher Power through meditation. Fourth, by reading about the spiritual quest, studying it through the words of others who have followed it throughout the centuries. Fifth, by practicing its principles in everyday life, by trying to live up to and expressing all that is fine and noble in our nature."

The quest is a three-fold path, my father explained to this lady, encompassing and developing feeling, intellect and character.

He went on to say that in one of his earlier books *The Secret Path* he had said that the quest could be summed up in one sentence, "Be still and know that I am God," but now he felt it necessary to add the other two dimensions of intellectual study and right action. All three are necessary.

And thus between the Sheepshead Bay and Flatbush Avenue stations on the BMT my father summed up what the quest is all about.

It was during this period that I remade the acquaintance of Anthony Damiani. We had first met in May 1947 when he and his wife, Ella May, came to Croton-on-Hudson for an interview with my father. "Tony" and I had liked each other at that first meeting but had gone our separate ways until now (1953). Tony, who was later to found Wisdom's Goldenrod (see Chapter 22) lived in Brooklyn and, as it turned out, only five minutes from where I lived myself. So I spent many evenings at the Damiani house listening to classical music and enjoying the delicious meals prepared by Ella May. In fact she used to give me a jar full of curried vegetables to take home for my next evening's dinner! I remember that Good Friday of 1954 when PB unexpectedly turned up on my doorstep whither he had been chauffeured by Anthony (as Tony was later to be called) and saying, "Come on, we're invited to a big dinner over at Tony's!" But in my immaturity I excused myself on the grounds that as it was a holy day I planned to spend it meditating, beating my breast, wearing my hairshirt, etc., etc. Whereupon my father smiled and quietly said, "It'll do you much more good to spend the time with me." Which I did.

My father for many years had a mailbox at the large post office on 42nd Street between Eighth and Ninth Avenues next to the then McGraw-Hill building. He had taken this because at the time (1954–1958) I was with the McGraw-Hill Publishing Company and he felt that this location would make it convenient for me to empty the box regularly and forward the mail to him wherever he might be in the world. The years 1955–1958 saw him traveling extensively in Europe, for instance. Following his instructions I would open and examine the incoming mail—for two reasons: first to lighten the forwarding weight by air mail, and second to send a brief form letter to the correspondents notifying them that Paul Brunton was out of the country and it might be several months before he would be able to attend to their letter. While this mailbox arrangement was indeed convenient as long as I was with McGraw-Hill, it became less so when I made a career move to Prentice Hall whose executive offices were at that time downtown in Greenwich Village on 13th Street and Fifth Avenue. And the location became decidedly inconvenient when we moved our company headquarters across the Hudson River to Englewood, New Jersey! But because the address, Box 339, Times Square Station, New York 36 New York, was so well known, PB preferred to maintain it. So I would make a weekly dash from my offices to drive over to Manhattan to reach the post office before it closed at 6:00 P.M.

My father was constantly inundated with letters from readers in addition to his regular correspondence with friends. In self-defense he devised a system of form letters to cover replies to people who read his books and then addressed him with all their personal problems. Here is a sample of such a form letter:

Your letter was carefully, sympathetically read.

However I regret that owing to advanced age, retirement from public activities and further withdrawal into spiritual retreat, it is no longer possible to reply directly to readers or give personal interviews; hence the need of this printed form.

Concerning your personal problem: have you tried to turn it over to the Higher Power? This is worth doing before using the normal human means open to you, and also after you have tried them.

Remember the Quest includes not only difficulties but also compensatory joys.

Peace and Light are the promise it holds if you persist to the end.

You have my benign thoughts for your inner welfare.

Yours, in Peace .

Paul Brunton

Many times my father would return a reader's letter to me, asking me to answer it on his behalf, which I did and always signed my letters "Mail Secretary."

Naturally I always sent my father a photocopy of their letter and a copy of my reply, and many times he would return it to me with scribbled comments for improvement. It was a good education, and of course I felt highly honored to be entrusted with such responsibility. I remembered that my father always ended his letters to readers with an uplifting final paragraph of positive endeavor—and I followed this same technique. Of course, if I felt unable to answer a reader's specific inquiry, I would forward it to my father accordingly. But nonetheless I felt flattered when my father would refer a New York reader to a meeting with me saying that I was well acquainted with his philosophy.

This was useful experience for me in learning to understand people's spiritual problems and on the more basic levels learning the sorts of things on which I could advise them and how to do so in the years to come, particularly after my father's death when I found myself led more and more into this field of service.

CHAPTER 14

PB's Mental Processes

If I now interject a personal note it is only because the background is necessary to illustrate a point.

In 1959, during my father's extended stay in New York, I fell in love with a young lady and wanted to marry her. Naturally I would not think of doing so without my father's blessing. PB agreed to meet us for dinner. The event turned out to be a calamity. My father was late in arriving at the restaurant and my lady friend was so nervous at the thought of meeting him that she filled the interval by drinking two martinis. Consequently she was not at her best for the occasion and to my surprise my father maintained silence almost throughout the meal. Next day when I went to see him to remark that the encounter had not been an unmitigated success, he replied, "What do you want from me? I could have indulged in chitchat if you like but I assumed you wanted me to ascertain whether she was suitable for you—and to do that I had to go within to the deeper part of my being and contact her intuitively."

This indicated that my father operated on two levels. Working through his ego on a normal everyday level his judgement would be, well, if not the same as yours and mine, nevertheless that of a very intelligent person; and it was possible for his judgement to be wrong and for him to make mistakes at this level. He could make bad judgements on minor matters just as you or I; many a time we went to see a bad movie!

But at the intuitive level when he got in touch with his Higher Self, then there could be no errors, no mistakes. This is the meaning of the Roman Catholic dogma that the Pope is incapable of moral error but is capable of mortal error.

My father told me that he could enter the realm of his Higher Self quite easily but that he had to become quiet to do so. This of course was not always practicable in the hustle and bustle of everyday life and so he was subject to the same stressful conditions as the rest of us.

Many people find this difficult to comprehend. They expect a person of my father's spiritual advancement to be perfect in every way and completely infallible. But this was not so, at least in my father's case. As he explained to me, "The spiritually enlightened person still has to work through his ego; except that the ego then becomes the servant rather than the master. But it is needed to function on this particular plane of existence."

People seem to believe that a person like my father could never have a negative thought; but of course he did, many of them—but he instantly squelched them and replaced them by a positive thought. Unlike the rest of us he never gave in to them. Or at least very seldom did he do so. Indeed I have seen my father angry: but then did not Jesus become angry when he drove the money changers out of the temple?

Returning to the story of my ill-fated engagement, at no time did my father specifically warn me against entering into this marriage. He left the decision to me. He even discussed with me where he and I should rent the formal attire required for the church wedding. Yet I suspect now that he knew it would never come about and was merely humoring me. As it happened I developed a bad cyst on my right eye, completely closing the lid so that I was unable to see out of the eye and went around wearing a pair of dark glasses. This should have warned me that I was not seeing the situation correctly! But I persisted in the illusion. Life itself trumped my cards when my fiancée broke off the engagement to marry someone else. Although I suffered ego-hurt at the time, later my father said to me, "You see how impossible the marriage would have been." And he was quite right. In fact many years later when I told my father that I felt he had dissuaded me from potential marriages on at least three occasions he replied, "Wouldn't you rather have me tell you what I think best for you in the long run? None of them would have worked out. You would only have ended up with unnecessary suffering." And he reminded me that he had told me years earlier that my astrological chart showed the need for caution in matters of the heart, that beneath the rose was a thorn. I must admit that time proved him right.

CHAPTER 15

Australia / New Zealand: 1960–63

In the fall of 1959 I helped PB pack his belongings at the Gramercy Park Hotel on 23rd Street in New York City where he had been staying and he left some of his suitcases with me in storage. I drove him out to Kennedy (then Idlewild) Airport and saw him off one rainy evening. Then I returned to the hotel and cleared his room of any remaining papers before handing in the key. Before he left, I had asked, "Won't you be lonely out there in Australia where you don't know anyone?"

"I am never lonely!" he smiled.

I said to my father, "We will miss you when you go."

"What do you mean?" he asked.

"Well, you know, the sheep will miss their shepherd."

"Oh, haven't you learned anything from me in all these years I've been trying to teach you!" he exclaimed. "I don't train sheep, I train shepherds!"

Little did I guess I was to visit him in Australia a few months later! It happened this way: a few weeks after his departure I was contacted by the US Department of State enquiring whether I would be willing to go out to Burma for six months to advise the national publishing company, Sarpey Beikman Institute, which had been founded by the then Prime Minister, U Nu. Apparently U Nu had inquired of the American Embassy in Rangoon whether a publishing specialist could be made available as an adviser. Enquiries were made and my name was duly proffered. Such are the intricacies of our destiny. When I wrote to my father about this invitation he urged me to accept it saying, "It will be good to balance your Western upbringing with some knowledge of the Orient."

The State Department had given me a first-class round-the-world ticket, but by expending a further four hundred dollars I was able to fly from Rangoon down to Perth where my father was living in Australia. And thus I was able to spend a week with him. This was less than six months after I had bid him goodbye at Idlewild Airport, little knowing when I would see him again!

My father had rented a house from a local bank manager who had gone with his family back to the mother country for some months. It was in a pleasant suburb, and my father liked Perth with its beautiful views of the harbor and quiet surroundings.

One evening we went to the university's theater and saw a play by George Bernard Shaw. My father enjoyed it and commented, "Although he always had a message, Shaw never forgot to be entertaining."

This visit, and the period in Burma prior to it, were also the occasion of an interesting story about my father's old friend Bud. While in Burma, I tried to find out about Bud's life there. I knew he had died a few years earlier. But it was not until a few days before I was due to depart that I was told about the two European monks living in the Swedagon Pagoda who might have known of this other foreigner, the Venerable Dorje Prajnananda. They knew my father for he had met them, together with Bud, during his trip to India in 1931. I went to visit them in their tiny quarters in the shadow of this large temple. They turned out to be the Latvian Archbishop of Buddhism and his disciple, Reverend Frederic Lustig. They shared their hut with dozens of stray cats! Yes, they had known Bud and took me to see the small hut in the center of a field where he had lived. I examined his minute quarters with interest. Then back at the monks' room they produced a small tin containing his ashes. They informed me that his last wishes were that half his ashes should be buried in Burma (and showed me the spot in the flower garden nearby where they had done so) and the remainder taken to England to be preserved in the headquarters of the Buddhist Society in London. They told me they had asked the General Secretary of that society, Mr Christmas Humphreys, during his visit to Rangoon to take the ashes back with him; but he had refused on the grounds, according to them, that it was bad luck to carry a dead man's ashes on a plane—that the plane would crash! I had no such qualms, however, and agreed to take the tin with me—whereupon my newly found Latvian friends took me by the hand and embarked upon a circular ritual dance. Round and round we went, with the candles flickering and the cats meowing. The scene is indelibly etched upon my memory!

Next morning I flew via Jakarta to Perth where my father was staying. But upon my arrival in Perth the burly Australian customs officer who inspected my baggage asked what was in the tin.

"A dead man's ashes," I told him. That seemed to perplex him: he was nonplussed.

"I've never had this before," he said. "Sorry, but I'll have to confiscate them and you can check with our headquarters in a few days."

When I did so I was told everything was now all right as the contents had been officially classified as "carbonized ashes!"

Then, while unpacking my suitcase, I found that the tin had not been securely fastened: some of the ashes had gotten loose and were all mixed up with my clothing. When I told my father this he said, "Well, there's only one thing to do. Take all your things out and then we'll have to vacuum the case." We did this, and then my father suggested we scatter the ashes around the flowers in the garden. So parts of Bud's earthly traces are in Perth as well as Rangoon and London.

I took the remainder of the ashes (more tightly fastened in

the tin!) around the world with me from Australia to Hong Kong and Japan before returning to the United States. When planning to make a business trip to England some months later, I wrote to the Buddhist Society and told them I would like to place the ashes in their shrine. Mr Humphreys replied that they did not feel they could accommodate my request. So I wrote back again on my business letterhead stating in an indignant tone that if they did not comply I would use every means at my disposal to broadcast the fact of their discourtesy to a gallant officer and outstanding Buddhist monk. This time the word came back that they would indeed accept the ashes. So upon arrival in London I telephoned them and made an appointment.

When I showed up at their offices in Eccleston Square two days later they were expecting me but Mr Humphreys was not there that day. Nevertheless, a pleasant lady greeted me and graciously ushered me into the inner sanctum. They had reserved a place of honor for the ashes, now put into a more suitable urn, and we placed them in this niche. We prostrated ourselves before the urn and each said our individual prayers. Thus was Bud's wish fulfilled.

I felt very proud to have been an agent in accommodating his desires in this matter.

A year later while I was living in India setting up a publishing company in New Delhi, I took the opportunity to visit my father again; this time he was living in a small rented house in Auckland, New Zealand. I spent a most enjoyable week there with him. He took me to see the large Polynesian Museum with its many well-preserved canoes and South Sea artifacts.

I remember one morning my father turning on his portable radio at breakfast and telling me about a local program whose presiding personality he enjoyed listening to. He had his human interests too.

My father liked New Zealand. He said its population had more book readers than Australia and the general atmosphere was more British. There was a metaphysical bookstore which he often frequented and subsequently he became friendly with its owners. Alas the store is long since out of business.

What was my father doing in Australasia? He resided in Perth, Sydney and Auckland for a combined period of three years. I feel it is now permissible to disclose the reason. He explained to me at the time that there were a handful of spiritually advanced people around the world whose mission it was to concentrate mentally during meditation upon the leaders of the chief nations. Their mission was to "pray for peace," to concentrate on raising the consciousness of the world's leaders to a level where their own higher selves could work on them for peace and restrain them from any rash warlike actions. He explained that this work was most effective if carried out in reasonable proximity to the geographical location of those leaders. I gathered that he had been allocated the task of mentally working upon Mao Zedong, the Chinese leader. The effectiveness of this overall work carried out during 1960 to 1962 may be gauged by the fact that the Cuban crisis, which occurred in October 1962, was indeed a critical flash-point for the world. As my father later explained to me, "Under normal circumstances, the events surrounding the Cuban confrontation would have led to all out nuclear war. But Grace intervened and gave humanity another chance." So the work of these spiritual people, in tune with the Universe, may be seen partly in that Mao Zedong did not take advantage of the Russians' preoccupation with the crisis to ferment his own territorial designs on the boundary with the USSR, partly in that John F. Kennedy and his brother Robert practiced restraint and tackled the emergency in a most professional manner, and partly in that Khrushchev took advantage of Kennedy's offering him a way out and backed down.

Who were these heavenly powers who assigned this task to my father and others? Well, he did not say but I refer the reader to his own description in the last chapter of *Discover Yourself (The Inner Reality)* wherein he describes the four celestial beings whose function it is to look after the evolution of this planet. It is interesting that the Roman Catholic Church also believes in four Archangels looking after this world— Uriel, Gabriel, Mikhail and Raphael. And Raphael was my father's given name!

I regret I cannot give more information about this matter. But is it not consoling that the heavenly powers enlist the aid of those who have reached the stage of development where they turn over their own life's purposes for the larger cause? And that the World Power itself is willing to give mankind every chance?

As my father explained to me:

This earthly plane is a school for gathering experience. A university of life. We are here to learn basic lessons, to cast off the vestiges of our animal ancestors and to get in tune with the infinite, to be at one with the universe. But when humanity refuses to obey the divine mandate for evolution and insists on following its own selfish materialistic ways, then there is no alternative but for the World-Mind to administer a rap across the knuckles, as it were—to give us a shock treatment, to make us query the meaning behind it and to change our ways. This has happened before, as witness Atlantis and Lemuria and Mu and it can happen again and it will if humanity does not change its course. We have been embroiled in two major world wars with all their attendant suffering and yet failed to see what lies behind them, the lessons we have to learn. Until we turn to the higher source and start living in our higher nature, such suffering is inevitable. As I wrote in my book *The Spiritual Crisis of Man* published in 1952, it seemed then that a cataclysm was bound to occur unless humanity changed course radically. I have seen no signs of it doing so. And by all events the Cuban crisis would normally have plunged us into yet another gigantic war. But the higher power decided to give us one more chance. It is up to us to seize this opportunity.

CHAPTER 16

The World Crisis: 1961

At this point I should explain that back in 1958 a number of my father's students were seriously planning to emigrate to Latin America to avoid a possible nuclear holocaust in the northern hemisphere. As early as 1952 my father had spoken of the likelihood of World War III occurring in 1962. He based his forecast on the fact that mankind evidently had not learned its lessons from the previous two world wars and needed yet another ghastly experience to force it to adopt the right course, the spiritual course. His thoughts appear in part in his *Notebooks*, Volume 9 (part 1):

> The refusal to recognize and apply this truth, that man is divine in essence and evolutionary goal—let alone its complete rejection—must bring disasters in the end, must provoke raging storms from time to time. (p. 253)

> If we make a comparison between our times and the conditions which preceded the destruction of the Greek and Roman civilizations, and if we note the chaos, dissension, strife, and violence which then prevailed and now prevail, we shall be forced to regard the future of our own civilization with apprehension. (p. 247)

Therefore he felt it prudent to warn his followers of this likely disaster. As he wrote in the same volume:

The clear Stoic perception of Marcus Aurelius Antonius lamented, "Rome is dying because Rome has nothing more to live for." But the awakened persons of today who refuse to yield to the animality and materialism of their epoch have something tremendously important to live for. They have escaped conquest by it because their own escape is to be the first fateful step towards achieving the future world-remnant's survival and escape. In doing so, in making their lone stand against this inner peril, they perform a valuable service of defense against the outer one. (p. 243)

Operation W.W.3: Its object is not to benefit certain persons while others, equally meritorious, remain unbenefitted, but to guard the higher philosophy and to preserve the Quest's practices and disciplines for generations yet to come. The benefit to individuals is incidental and due in most cases to favourable karma created by devoted service. (p. 253)

He felt in those years that those who could leave the danger zones owed it to future generations, no less than to themselves, to do so and thereby preserve the spiritual teachings of the quest for the postwar period. Latin America seemed the closest refuge for those living in the United States as the scientific belief of the fifties (later revised) was that prevailing winds would carry nuclear fallout horizontally around the northern hemisphere. So many of us decided to move to the southern half of the globe. As Ecuador and Brazil were our favored countries, I spent time in 1959 at their Washington embassies gathering information about living conditions. Indeed two married couples and a single quester did actually proceed down there and obtained employment and stayed for a few years—until after they received their copies of *The Message*.

The Message was a document PB dictated to me in March 1961 during my visit to him in Perth, Australia. We had been discussing the world situation when he suddenly exclaimed, "But it's all different now! Operation Shield no longer applies now and I must tell them about the new situation and the spiritual meaning of the world crisis." We spent the remainder of the day assembling *The Message*—PB walking back and forth dictating while I took it down in my rusty shorthand and then pecked away at his portable typewriter. Several drafts were revised before my father was satisfied with the final composition.

The Message—March 1961

1. *International Situation.* There is a great change in the world situation during the past eighteen months. There seems to be no real danger this year but as you know I used to say that 1962 might be a critical year. That is still true, but I do not now believe that Khrushchev wants war while he can continue the cold war. His scientific advisers have frightened him with their picture of what war would mean to the world including Russia—and to both antagonists if war did happen. The real danger lies in the fanaticism, materialism and ruthlessness of one man, Mao Tse-tung, who is definitely aggressively minded. But since he is not equipped to start a war, and could not be before two years at the very least, and four to five years in the opinion of some experts, it may well be that 1962 will also not be in real danger. There is also a possibility that he and Khrushchev may part company.

2. *Operation Shield.* All previously held opinions on the comparative safety of various areas must be revised radically. These opinions were based on the fallout data available at that time—but such data was predicated on the basis of the nuclear tests. The scientific results of the International Geophysical Year now available show that we can no longer proceed on this premise. Scientists agree that in

event of war the entire planetary system would be flooded
with radioactivity because of the immense quantities
thrown into the atmosphere. Thus there is no longer any
certainty of safety from fallout anywhere in the world. This
is a day of judgement for the *whole* world. Further, the use
being made by Russia of Castro to spread communism in
SA will undoubtedly increase and develop, along with his
anti-American activities. The dangers of mob violence in
many SA countries has, and will increase. However, SA
will certainly be less of a bomb target than the USA, if
indeed it is one at all. There is no solution as such for a safe
location. I no longer recommend any place. However, there
is a partial solution. Scientists agree that breaks would occur in the world-wide radioactive coverage which would
provide areas of safety, but they cannot foretell where these
breaks would be. Also, to minimize the danger of total
world destruction, both antagonists are likely to employ
"clean" bombs to reduce the amount of radioactive fallout
hurled into the planetary system. And the Chinese, who
need living space to accommodate their over-population,
would employ these clean bombs against targets and large
cities to leave large areas available for colonization. Thus,
the radius of effectiveness of a clean bomb being 30 miles, if
one can reside at least 30 miles or more from a possible
target, the odds in favour of comparative safety are tremendously increased. About one third of the world's population will be saved to carry on if a war comes, including
many from the northern hemisphere, including indeed the
USA, Europe and Russia.

3. *The Real Solution*. In the past we have acted on the premise that the saving of one's life would allow longer time to
make headway on the quest. But this is long path thinking,
and also places too much emphasis on the physical survival
of the body. Our purpose for being on earth is a spiritual
one; therefore the only true solution must likewise be a

spiritual one. We have seen above that there will be areas of safety throughout the world; it will lie in the will of God, and to some extent our personal karma, whether the area where one is living is protected by a break in the atmosphere or not. Therefore the only practical solution to Operation Shield, the only real safety, is complete dependence on the Higher Power. This, of course, entails application of the short path: the cutting of the Gordian knot of the long path with its preoccupation with the faults of the ego. Needless to say, and more importantly, this solution provides also the opportunity for hastened spiritual advancement as well as survival.

4. *An Opportunity for Questers.* There comes a time on this path when questers are given the opportunity to stand on their own feet and show what they have absorbed from the teachings. It is an inevitable period which has to come and is to be negotiated. Everything is subject to change, as Gautama taught, and PB's role is no longer the same. We can't go on as though things were the same; the relationship must undergo change—for the quester's benefit and for his work. For some years he had been edging into semi-retirement and is now going into deeper retirement for the time being. Eventually he hopes to see all the questers again when this phase is over—but he cannot do so now nor can he get involved in correspondence or answering personal or spiritual questions. He has to be outwardly away and free to attend to his personal assignment which involves the fate of millions. He cannot allow himself to be distracted by the few and they should not be so selfish as to expect him to. "Has he deserted us just at the critical time when we need him most? What are we to do?" That's just the point: just when they (seem to) need him most is the indicated time for them to stand on their own feet, to develop the use of their own faculties. It could not be otherwise, and both we and PB must obey this inevitable law. We

can find the real PB within ourselves. "Realization means understanding by yourself." There is a strong current today in such a critical time as this, a current leading to the Higher Power. With such an unprecedented threat menacing the entire world, because of yang and ying, there comes also an unprecedented opportunity for speedy spiritual advancement. We can make greater strides in this lifetime than we could in dozens of other lifetimes put together. Sooner or later we have to get down to the business of finishing the path—it does have an end—and we mustn't think it beyond our reach. PB is the example that it *can* be done. The short path techniques, coupled with this spiritual current, can carry us to realization in *this* lifetime—if we make up our minds accordingly. And, even if we do not make the final grade, the efforts and progress we do make will be invaluable for the next incarnation. And, of course, these same efforts will help provide the karma and safety in the international situation, as previously explained in paragraph 3.

Summary: There are no longer any certainties. It is impossible to predict the outcome of present activities for peace and to say whether or not the future will be bright or dark. The only real security today is dependence on God. Everything is in a state of delicate balance and the final result may even be some years off, whether for good or bad.

In this unsettled situation, PB regrets he is not able to give advice. He will make no further predictions; we have the facts and must resolve them for ourselves. (Unless he comes across new scientific data, etc., which he will pass on. Likewise, if he received a definite revelation regarding time and place, he will pass it on but he does NOT expect it.)

Now is the time, the opportunity to make rapid progress. And we can only make it by being left to stand on our own feet.

Nevertheless, PB never forgets those who do not forget him. And the inner tie is the most important.

So I brought *The Message* back to the States with me, made photocopies and mailed them with a cover note to questers living in Europe. For those living in the New York area I gave them out and discussed *The Message* with them. Among these were Ella May and Anthony Damiani, Teruko and Bert Salmirs and a few other questers all living in Brooklyn at that time. It's interesting to note how the hand of Fate works: if the Damianis had emigrated to Ecuador (they actually bought land there as a preparatory move), would there then ever have been a Wisdom's Goldenrod Center for Philosophic Studies, the organization Anthony later founded in upstate New York, and which plays such an important role in the lives of its members? But "Que sera, sera!"

So we took *The Message* to heart and dropped our plans for migrating to Latin America. Rereading it twenty-seven years later, one sees that PB's prophecy of China and Russia parting company soon came about, and that 1962 with its Cuban crisis did indeed prove a critical year. And the final paragraphs of point four are as vital today as they were in 1961 and still well worth reflecting over.

CHAPTER 17

New York: 1964

My father returned to the United States from his long sojourn in Australia and New Zealand in 1964. He sublet an apartment on East 33rd Street in New York City, not far from where I had taken an apartment upon my return a year earlier from India. This enabled me to see a lot of him. We often had dinner together, usually at a restaurant, either with friends or just the two of us.

One day PB expressed a wish to visit my offices located over in Englewood Cliffs, New Jersey. So one Saturday morning I picked him up and we drove over the George Washington Bridge to the corporate headquarters of Prentice-Hall, Inc. I showed my father the premises and he admired the oriental *objets d'art* with which I had furnished my office.

We then sat together at my long conference table and spent the rest of the morning reviewing the many corrections my father wished effected in the next printings of his various books. These were partly typographical errors but mostly were changes he wished made either to clarify a point or because he had changed his view on the matter in question. We then divided these lists of changes into two groups: important and essential ones, and those which while desirable were not vital. My father then asked me to take up this matter of changes with both his British and American publishers. This in due course I did, and found them both amenable to making the short list of important changes while reserving the longer list for such time as they might do a complete new typesetting of the book in question. However with books which had been in print for more than twenty years, the latter was not likely. And indeed the changes have yet to be implemented fully.

But back to that morning in July 1964. As we left my office to go to lunch my father remarked upon the quiet surroundings, pleasantly wooded. "Why don't you consider living over here?" he asked. "It's so much more restful than Manhattan."

"Oh, I like to be in the center of things and close to theaters, the opera, restaurants," I replied.

"But over here you have trees and you'd be so much closer to your office and wouldn't have to drive to and fro in all that traffic every day," he persisted.

At that moment about half a mile from my office, we happened to pass a new six-story apartment building with a large "Renting Now" sign displayed. "Why don't we take a look?" PB asked? I demurred. "It won't hurt just to take a look," he said.

Well, you can guess the rest of the story. We emerged from the building an hour later after my having signed a two-year contract on a nice corner apartment on the sixth floor with a spectacular view of the George Washington Bridge. Of course, my father was quite right, it *was* better living in New Jersey and much more convenient being so close to my office. I could still visit New York City in the evenings for the opera and theater and all in all it was a very good move.

Then my father surprised me by saying, "Well, this is your first completely unfurnished apartment. Why don't we go and look for some furniture for it?"

Why not, indeed, and off we went to the nearest shopping mall where, would you believe it, my father spotted a pair of end table lamps whose bases were fashioned in Buddha heads! He examined them closely and said they were a good facsimile of a Cambodian Buddha even to the coiled snake on the forehead. I still have those lamps and treasure them for that memory as well as for their beauty. My father not only helped me furnish my new apartment, but also helped me with the moving. He came to my old apartment and helped me pack. But I suspect looking back many years later, that he used such occasions as opportunities for us to be together and for him to relax from the pressure of his other duties.

Father and son...PB at 35 and myself at 10, 1933.

My mother, Karen Augusta Tottrup, age 53, 1952.

*My godfather, Brother M (Mr Thurston),
an advanced occultist...*

*and Alan Bennett
(Ananda Metteya)...*

the two early spiritual influences on PB.

In the 1930s...

PB typing on his trusty portable in India...

and handling snakes in Egypt.

India, 1942.

*"Bud", the Venerable
Dorje Prajnanda in
Burma.*

Sri Ramana
Maharshi

PB at the Ramana
Ashram.

PB while lecturing in Los Angeles, seen here with Dan Franz and
another student, 1938.

Dear Kenny: 14 Sept 43
        Here are two photographs sent as requested and mentioned
in my airgraph of early September 43. Both are recent.
        (1) was taken without my knowledge by my secretary
        whilst I was at work writing on the flat roof of my house

        (2) was taken by an official photographer at a Goverment
        function as part of a group, from which it is cut out.

        The photos Mother and you sent me of yourself still
show naval uniform. Havent you one with an airman's uniform?
If so, I'd like to have it. Surely you dont go up in the air
with those wide flapping trousers of a jolly Jack tar!

                                        affectionately
                                            Paul

from Dr. PAUL BRUNTON
    c/o Thos. Cook & Son Ltd
    Postbox 171, Madras, India

For Kenny:
With affectionate regards,
Paul 1943

PB in his early forties, with his favorite Parker fountain pen.

PB disliked posing for photographs, as evidenced by his stern expression!

My father posing for me in the garden, One Observatory Drive, Croton-on-Hudson, New York in 1947.

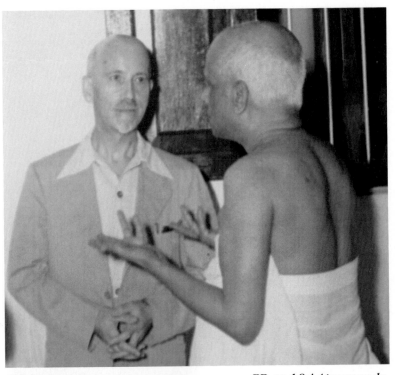

PB and Sri Atmananda.

*Taken in Copenhagen in 1952
by Evangeline Glass.*

*Milano, with Erna
Rosa King.*

*My father dressed
elegantly when he
chose to.*

In Erna Rosa King's apartment in Verona, Italy, 1965.

The author took both these snaps in Switzerland.

Age 66.

1975

PB taking his ease.

PB delighted in his custom horseshoe desk! *Photo:* Alfred Ras

Switzerland.

The author giving a public lecture on PB in 1988.

Photo: James E. Jeffries

Snapped in Lugano by Dr Arthur Broekhuysen.

During the last years of his life, PB appeared almost translucent, radiating inner light.

A few months before his transition, 1981.

CHAPTER 18

England: 1965

My father left New York in late 1964 to travel across the country visiting friends and students. He returned to New York in the spring of 1965 and stayed for a few weeks in the apartment of Edmund Luescher on 106th Street near Broadway. Edmund was Swiss but lived in the USA. He had written PB two years earlier and, as Edmund lived in New York, PB sent me his letter and asked me to meet with him. (As mentioned earlier, PB did this with many correspondents who were in the New York area, together with those in other countries when he felt I could answer them.) Edmund had read PB's books for many years and was vice president of a large importer of machinery from Europe. I had tea with Edmund one Saturday, after which I gave a favorable report on him to PB and suggested that PB grant him an interview upon his next visit to New York—which he did.

A widower, Edmund lived in a large, well-constructed apartment. I visited there several times during PB's stay. I remember once going out shopping for salad items, returning and preparing the luncheon; another evening the three of us went out to a Chinese restaurant nearby. As we were returning to the apartment and crossing Broadway, PB was talking about people with weight problems. Suddenly looking at me he commented upon my girth and said, "Kenneth is just on the verge."

That summer (1965) PB went to London, rented a flat, and settled in for a lengthy stay. I went over in September and spent two weeks there, staying as I usually did with my mother and stepfather in Enfield, a suburb on the fringe of North London. I spent several days with PB. One day he expressed a wish to see the area where he and my mother had lived and where I was born. So we took a bus to Highgate and walked across a park to Parliament Hill Fields. He showed me the house they had lived in. It was still standing in good condition. Then we caught a bus to the top of the hill to Hampstead, an area which my father liked. Originally a village on the outskirts of London it affords a good view of the city proper. Today, as in my father's youth, it is a center for artistic people, writers, artists. It has developed into a comfortable quarter for the well-to-do. My father liked its cosmopolitan atmosphere and its many little boutiques and bookstores. We wandered around, browsed in the windows, had traditional tea in a little tea room, and then later went to a vegetarian restaurant called "Pippins" for dinner. I now stay at a hotel in Hampstead whenever I visit London and retrace the steps of that day in 1965 and conjure up its memories.

Another evening by arrangement, I took PB out to have dinner with my mother and stepfather at their home. It proved a pleasant evening with much warm reminiscing by the three. It had been nearly thirty years since the three of them, and indeed the four of us, had been together.

CHAPTER 19

Portugal: 1966

In 1966 my father was staying in Zollikerberg, a suburb of Zurich, Switzerland. He wrote and suggested that we meet and take a vacation together in Portugal. Accordingly I flew to Zurich to meet him and the next day we flew together to Lisbon. I had arranged for a car rental there and we drove south from the airport to the coast known as the Algarve. We passed a pleasant week staying here a night, there a night. Together we stood on the westernmost promontory of Portugal where Prince Henry the Navigator had gazed out upon the stormy Atlantic. We wandered amid small fishing villages, were met with unfailing politeness, and were always able to obtain vegetarian cuisine.

One evening in the town of Lagos we had finished our dinner at the hotel and were strolling in the gardens outside. Suddenly my father asked, "Do you have a pencil and paper on you?" I replied yes and fished them out of my pocket, ready to take down his dictation.

He continued, "I want to make a list of bequests of personal items to be left to various people after my death."

I was somewhat shaken to say the least, but I held my pencil at readiness to fulfill this strange request.

He then proceeded to reel off a list of names, most of whom I had met, but others whom I only knew by name. He took considerable care in deciding what item he would give to each: for one a pair of gold cuff links, for another, a jade ring, and so on, until about twenty names had been identified together with their appropriate gift.

During the next few days he would refer to this list and ask to see it. He would examine it carefully and revise some of the bequests. He asked me to type up the list when I returned to the States, send him a copy, and be prepared to undertake to find the various items and ensure that they reached their rightful legatees.

When the time came I was able to carry out his wishes except that by then, fifteen plus years later, a few of the individuals had made their own transitions. One or two individuals were hard to locate, but eventually I managed to track them all down and present them with the appropriate memento from PB. I have already described how I managed to locate Joseph Bevine in London. Another person, Myron (Dan Franz) had died some years before my father; in this case I presented the beautiful jade Buddha designated for him to his son Mike and daughter-in-law Jane, living in California.

Coincidentally during my last visit with my father in February 1981 I was able to give him a handsome red sweater which Jane Franz had sent to me to forward to him. So I took it with me on my next visit. He liked it; in fact, one afternoon as we were going out for tea he asked, "Shall I wear the new red jumper?" A few months later after his transition I took back the sweater and returned it to Jane.

Following Lagos, we drove back to Lisbon and stayed for a few days at the Hotel Ritz, a lovely large hotel appointed in the old-world manner. We discovered a quaint vegetarian restaurant, located in a residential building and with no more than half a dozen tables.

On the second day however my father fell ill and decided to stay in bed. That evening he asked me to get him some bottles of fruit juice when I visited the same restaurant for my evening meal. I hurried back with them and PB drank them eagerly to quench his fevered thirst. But the next morning when I went to his room he felt worse. He had abstained from solid foods, but he said he should have omitted the juices also to give the body energies a chance for a complete healing cure unimpeded by any digestive process. He pointed out that this is what animals do when they become ill—curl up in a corner and refuse food or liquid. I stayed by his bed that day as he slept. Frankly I was becoming somewhat concerned. He seemed so still and quiet. He refused to see the hotel doctor, saying the body would heal itself.

I was due to fly back to New York in a couple of days and began wondering if I would have to postpone my return. The next morning dawned cheerful to find him sitting up and recovered, fully recovered. But, whether from sympathy or because I had caught the same virus, I just as quickly came down with a fever and had to retire to my bed in the adjoining room. Some friends came to visit PB and then went to dinner with him. By next morning I had recovered sufficiently to make my flight and the friends accompanied my father and me to the airport. PB's plane was due to depart later that afternoon and they assured me they would see him safely on it. So I flew back to New York and he flew back to Zurich. Yet another memorable vignette in the host of memories shared from our intertwined lifetimes.

Here is a letter PB wrote me shortly after:

In view of your sickness at Lisbon, I hope to hear of your recovery when you next write dear Kenneth —

Shall leave Switzerland in a few days time, so please hold all mail until I can furnish the next address.

Your help and service in Portugal made me grateful, being so extensive and devoted. Never mind about the interruptions which prevented realisation of the projected program in meditation: Your inner development will work out just the same in the end. Be patient and a little more hopeful.

Please give kindest good wishes to Edmund

With Peace + affection

PB.

3 November 1965

CHAPTER 20

Tea and Other Matters

Italy: 1968

Turin

While I was visiting my father in Switzerland later in 1968 he said, "Why don't we go to Turin in Italy for a few days? It will make a break." So next morning we took the train and arrived in time for lunch at the big hotel opposite the railway station in Turin. Here we obtained a good green salad meal. That evening we discovered a restaurant named Lux which we subsequently patronized for lunch and dinner every day during the rest of our stay. The chef went out of his way to prepare vegetarian meals for us and managed to come up with many variations of pasta and vegetables. My father commented upon the name of the restaurant as being highly appropriate!

We liked Turin and enjoyed meandering through its tree-lined streets and browsing among its shopping arcades. As always my father was particularly interested in bookstores and would examine volumes in several languages. Stationary stores interested him too; he was always keen to examine the latest models in ballpoint pens. We would seek out different tea shops each day and order Indian tea, with extra hot water, and toast and honey. PB seldom varied this selection although occasionally he would indulge in some plain cake. He never overcame his inbred British taste for tea in the late afternoon;

this of course meant that we tended to dine at a later hour, certainly later than my American habits were used to. At home my father would take a rest after luncheon, and following his siesta would reappear and start preparing the kettle and teapot for his daily ritual. When we had tea out it was always necessary to request extra hot water to dilute the strength of the tea. My father had been an *aficionado* of tea since his youth. He often referred to it as "the cup that cheers but does not inebriate." In fact he blamed his subsequent varicose veins in later years on his habit of drinking black tea late at night when he had work to accomplish. In his later years he switched from black to green tea, particularly the Japanese variety, and whenever I visited Japan he asked me to bring him some. He also asked me to bring him a small wooden tea holder to use instead of the normal aluminum or steel infusers for the loose leaves; this was long before such holders became available in the West. He knew instinctively that metal affected the taste of tea, whereas wood did so to a much lesser extent. His favorite black tea was a Chinese blend, Lapsang Souchong, which emits a delightful misty smoky fragrance. He was also fond of Jasmine tea. I remember once when I was visiting Paris he asked me to seek out a wholesaler on the Left Bank to obtain a blend called *Fleurs de Thé* which was somewhat similar to Jasmine. He enjoyed having tea out at high-class tea shops or restaurants. While he lived in Switzerland, his favorite was Zurchers in Montreux with large windows overlooking Lake Geneva, sparkling linen tablecloths, and gleaming cutlery. Not only was an excellent tea available there, but he particularly enjoyed the music rendered by a violinist whose wife accompanied on the piano. They played light classical renditions and the whole effect was a most agreeable ambiance. So after a walk along the lakefront to feed the ducks and swans with bread from his pockets we would repair to this tea shop for an enjoyable repast.

Tea memoirs of my father would not be complete without

mentioning that when he was staying with me in May 1977 at my home in Nyack I returned from the office one day to find that he had removed all my various brands of tea (which I used to buy wholesale in Greenwich Village) from their paper containers and placed them in glass jars, neatly lettering the kind of tea on paper and taping it to the outside of the jar! He pointed out that this would maintain the tea's freshness longer. He was quite correct too!

During World War II when tea was rationed in Great Britain he sent a wooden container of Darjeeling tea safely packaged with silver foil to my mother. This lasted us a long time!

My father enjoyed the atmosphere of Turin. And he liked the Piedmontese people of the region. He felt they were intelligent and courteous above the ordinary. It was in Turin that he spotted a man's suit in a tailor's window. He liked it and accepted when I offered to buy it for him. It was an attractive lightweight brown suit which he was quite proud of and wore often.

Rome

Although I visited Rome several times on my own business affairs, I was there only once together with my father. It happened like this.

I received a cablegram in February 1968 from my father stating he was grievously ill in the American hospital in Rome and not expected to live so he felt it advisable that I should go there as soon as possible.

I immediately put my affairs in order, took a plane to Rome, and went directly to the hospital—where I was greatly relieved to find PB sitting up in bed in his private room and cheerfully announcing that he had had an almost miraculous recovery. He told me that the unknown malady which had struck him a few weeks earlier had caused him to be unable to swallow any food. He had been taken ill in his hotel room and had been so weak that he was unable to summon help. Eventually he was discovered by the chambermaid and the hotel manager in turn arranged for him to be removed to the hospital. They chose the American hospital because of its English-speaking personnel.

I stayed with my father four days and nights, continually by his side. He was allowed out of bed for his meals and we took these together in a small dining room. I still recall sitting by his bedside looking up at him and over his head through the window while the lights of St Peters and the Vatican twinkled. When I left to return to the States he was well on the road to recovery.

I can recall only three other illnesses (other than those already mentioned) of my father's. In the 1950s he suddenly suffered from an attack of what he later told me was black magic, a spell put on him by an Indian fakir. Let him relate it in his own words, as they appear on page 61 of *Reflections*, Volume 8 in his *Notebooks*:

> It was the opening of summer in 1953. An internal tropi-cal malady caught from eating deliberately poisoned food a few months earlier in the Far East had run its course and was about to end, as it so often did end, fatally. I suddenly and involuntarily fell across the writing desk and felt con-sciousness slumping into a coma. I dragged myself some-how to a couch and there the coma turned out to be the death swoon. After a couple of moments I was already almost entirely out of the physical body. The line was about to be drawn to close the past lifetime's account. . . . In that condition and at that moment my body was found by some-one who happened to enter the room, someone so highly sensitive and intuitive as to recognize at once what the hidden situation was. My friend called me to come back, emphatically, pleadingly, and insistently by turns. At the same time I awoke to a dreamy consciousness, half in one world, where the astral figure of a Master, well-known and well-loved, appeared to me, and half in the physical world.

The Master said, "I have come to take you away. But you still have the choice, whether to return or to come with me." I reflected rapidly. Personally I felt quite willing to accept the vast relief from the burden of PB's earthly life now offered me. But at the same time, I felt pity for those who looked to me for help. The work with and for them was unfinished. My mission to them and to others was unfulfilled. How could I go? All this happened in a very few seconds. Regretfully, reluctantly, the decision formed itself within my heart. I asked to be allowed to return to the flesh so that I could continue the service and complete the record.

He also suffered periodically from a debilitating illness called sprue. This is a chronic disease of the tropics marked by anemia, emaciation and gastro-intestinal disturbances. My father picked it up from living in India throughout the war years.

And of course there was his final stroke and coma which I shall relate later.

CHAPTER 21

New York: 1977

My father spent the month of May in 1977 staying with me at my home in Nyack, New York.

While I was at my office he often passed the day seated at the writing desk in my study overlooking the Hudson River. On other days he would wish to spend the day in Manhattan so I would drive him to the train station in the morning, or if he wished to go later he would take a taxi and I would drive over to New York in the evening and meet him. Most often our rendezvous was at the Farm Food Vegetarian Restaurant on West 49th Street between Broadway and Sixth Avenue, which had long been a favorite of ours. We had both been regular patrons since my arrival in New York thirty years before. PB was particularly fond of their Creole vegetable soup and the thick black bread served with it. This would be followed by one of the soy nutroast entrées, a baked potato and steamed carrots. (Carrots were a great favorite of my father's: in his later years he would have them raw, sliced or diced in his midday salad, and again with his cooked vegetables in the evening.) He would have a fruit cup for dessert while my favorite was the butterscotch pudding. Then we would walk around for an hour or so, looking in the shop windows and discussing this and that. He liked to relax after having occupied all day with giving interviews to people in the city, usually at someone's home, or going on various errands (such as seeking out an old-time pharmacy like Kiehl's down on Third Avenue between 13th and 12th Streets where he purchased homeopathic medication unavailable elsewhere).

During one such evening's peregrinations we stopped at a bookstore on Fifth Avenue where I purchased a copy of Alan Watts' *Zen and the Art of Archery*. When we got home we sat at my kitchen table and read portions of the book. PB expressed his opinion that Watts had made an important contribution to opening Western readers' eyes to Oriental philosophy, particularly to Japanese Zen. But he felt that Watts' overindulgence in alcohol had dulled his inner sensitivity to the mystical life.

Another evening, while staying with me during the same period, he expressed a desire to read something light to take to bed with him.

"How about the *Bhagavad Gita*?" I suggested.

"No, no," he said, "'I want something *light*!"

"Well, how about Madame Blavatsky?" I asked.

"No, no! I mean *light*!"

After browsing through my bookshelves PB settled for a collection of Ray Bradbury stories!

My father enjoyed talking about writers and books. He admired G.K. Chesterton, Charles Morgan (especially his novel *The Fountain*), Algernon Blackwood's tales of the occult, Bulwer-Lytton whose *Zanoni* fascinated him as a teenager, and Arnold Bennett, among others, for their literary ability. I can recall vividly the summer evening in Corseaux, Switzerland, when after dinner in his apartment we sat in the dusk and PB reminisced about authors and their works. When the time came to return to my hotel he saw me to the door and remarked with a smile, "I enjoyed our literary causerie!"

In Hollywood in 1938 PB met Somerset Maugham at a dinner party. The novelist became interested in my father's recounting how he had gone to India six years earlier to seek out holy men who could impart spiritual truth to him. As PB later told me: "Maugham was a true professional novelist; everything was grist for his mill." Maugham sensed the possibility of a story and so he in turn traveled to India and traced PB's footsteps to the Ramanashram. When he was ushered into the presence of Ramana Maharshi the heat overpowered him and he fainted. "The disciples claimed that Maugham had gone into a *samadhi* trance," related PB, "but in actuality it was only the heat combined with a physical condition of Maugham's."

PB was an ardent visitor to public libraries wherever he might be—whether the giant New York City main library, or a rural local library in Brookfield, Connecticut, or the English-language library in Vevey in the shade of Nestle's world head-quarters, or the reading rooms of the British Museum in London. He enjoyed browsing through the periodicals and scanning the recent magazines and papers. I accompanied him on many such visits and he kindled in me a lifelong love for and appreciation of such media service centers.

CHAPTER 22

Wisdom's Goldenrod

PB's Last U.S. Trip

I have previously referred to my friend, Anthony Damiani. In 1962 he and his wife Ella May moved from Brooklyn to upstate New York. He told me they wanted a better environment in which to bring up their children, but he also was responding to a deeper inner call. He obtained a position as a toll collector from the New York Thruway and deliberately chose night duty to allow him time to study. He then opened a small bookstore in downtown Ithaca specializing in occult and philosophical works. He put a large sign "Astrology" in the window which attracted many students from nearby Cornell University and Ithaca College.

The 1960s were the years of the flower children at colleges across America. Many young people were rebelling against the restraints imposed by conventional society and were seeking meaning and inner peace beyond that offered by orthodox religions. Anthony's astrology classes drew some of them into the store, where they soon found themselves studying various other philosophic and spiritual subjects under his tutelage. He was a firm taskmaster and would not allow any drug-taking among those who wanted to study with him; indeed nearly all of those who chose to do so promptly emulated his own vegetarian diet. As the group increased in size, the tiny store (named "The American Brahman") bulged at the seams during evening classes. After considering various options, Anthony settled on the idea of erecting a building on land he owned adjoining his home. This location would provide both more space for his classes and a retreat in quiet country surroundings for his students. The setting is idyllic: overlooking Seneca Lake, nestled in the heart of the wine-growing country of the Finger Lakes area, it reflects a rare degree of peace and tranquility.

In 1971 Anthony accepted the offer from one of his students, Andrew Holmes, an English teacher at the local high school, to design and supervise the physical construction of the main building. Dozens of students pitched in to erect the large log chalet which still stands solidly today and is used as the Center's main building and meditation hall.

As the group's size approached two hundred students, the need for a proper organizational footing became evident. Wisdom's Goldenrod Center for Philosophic Studies was duly formed and granted tax-free status as a non-profit organization. Regular evening classes were enthusiastically attended by students who drove out from Ithaca (twenty-two miles to the east) as well as a number of local people from the immediate community.

In 1977 a second building was erected to accommodate out-of-town guests and provide a refuge for weekend retreats. In short order two more buildings were constructed. One was a library beautifully fashioned in the shape of a Bhutanese temple and today containing an outstanding collection of volumes on philosophical, mystical and spiritual subjects, Hinduism, Buddhism, etc., attractively displayed. Dedicated by the Dalai Lama in 1979, the building has an aura of serenity conducive both to contemplative study and meditation; it is a treat for many to spend an afternoon studying among its archives. The fourth building, now named "The Annex," today houses the manager of the Center. Downstairs is used as a workplace for the Paul Brunton Philosophic Foundation Notebooks Project.

The entrance to the parklike grounds of Wisdom's Goldenrod lies off Route 414 in Valois, ten miles north of Watkins Glen. One enters from the parking area by passing through a large Japanese Tori and then crossing a wooden bridge over a flowing stream into the main grounds. All of the construction (except for digging and pouring foundations) and all of the landscaping was done on a volunteer basis by members of Wisdom's Goldenrod.

Anthony Damiani was a dedicated student of my father's philosophy. His own classes at the Center included commentaries on and discussion of my father's works, together with those of Plotinus, Plato, Jung, and representatives of all major religio-philosophical traditions—most notably the Hindu, Buddhist, and Greek traditions. He wrote to my father regularly about what he was doing and what he was trying to accomplish.

Although there were other groups studying my father's books around the world, they were small, and my father expressed concern about this group of nearly two hundred students. So in 1972 he asked me to visit Wisdom's Goldenrod and check it out. This I did. I stayed at Anthony's house, attended the classes, had some long walks and talks with Anthony—and subsequently turned in a favorable report to my father.

My second visit came unexpectedly after suffering a heart attack three years later. Upon my release from the hospital Anthony sent down for me; a mutual friend and member of his group, Gillian Pederson-Krag, came to Nyack and drove me the two hundred and fifty miles upstate to Valois. This time I stayed a month resting and convalescing in Anthony's home. We had long talks daily and became very close during this period. Anthony and Ella May often drove me around the countryside to show me the sights. (Little did I know then that thirteen years later, I myself would have a summer home constructed here by the same master builder who built the Center, Andrew Holmes.)

Anthony repeatedly invited my father to stay for an extended period, if not live altogether, at the Center and offered to put the guest cottage at my father's disposal. I too encouraged my father in this regard for with his advancing age I felt it prudent for him to have close friends nearby. And indeed the students at the Center would have taken care of all his housekeeping and culinary requirements. But PB prized his independence and privacy to the end. In 1977, however, he finally agreed to visit Wisdom's Goldenrod during an extended visit to the United States.

He arrived in New York April 30 on Queen Elizabeth II and stayed a month with me at my home in Nyack. On May 30 Anthony drove down, stayed the night with us, and next morning drove PB up to Valois. The guest house on the grounds was not yet completed. After inspecting several options, PB decided to stay at the nearby home of Bert and Teruko Salmirs, and it was here that he granted more than one hundred interviews to members of the Center. Many of these interviews were recorded by those involved, and I hope that in the near future they will be published by the Paul Brunton Philosophic Foundation so that all may share his remarks.

After a month in Valois he returned to New York City and then promptly set off on a cross-country journey with stops in the midwest. He spent two weeks with a Goldenrod-related group in Columbus, Ohio, and a month in California before returning to New York to spend a few more weeks with me before returning to Europe.

During that time, I used to look forward to leaving the office as promptly as possible and speeding home to have tea with PB. I was undergoing a difficult ordeal in my business career and he provided invaluable advice and encouragement.

On the night before his departure I received a replica statue of the Goddess Selket, one of a hundred made to order by the Metropolitan Museum of Art in conjunction with the Tutankhamen exhibition at that time. PB helped me unpack the statue and I was at a loss where to put this enormous thirty-eight inch high gold figure with its outspread arms.

"Why not put it in the middle of your Buddha collection?"
he asked. "After all she is the Egyptian goddess of protection
and they used her for this purpose in Tutankhamen's tomb."

"Well I hope she guards my Buddhas better than she did
Tutankhamen," I replied.

"Ah, but look what happened to those who invaded Tutankhamen's tomb," my father pointed out. "They all came to
a sticky end!"

And so Lady Selket was duly installed in the midst of my
Buddhas and has guarded them ever since.

Next morning I helped my father pack his suitcases; but it
soon became obvious that there were many papers for which
there was no room in the cases.

"Don't worry," I said, "I'll have the office mail these to you."
And so he left them for me to forward later.

We drove out to JFK airport and checked in at Swissair. I
was handling my father's ticket and passport at the check-in
counter and when I turned around he had disappeared! Well,
I kept my cool and went looking for him. When I finally found
him I said, "I thought something like this might happen."

"Oh, you did, did you—then you're learning!" was my
father's reply.

As I took him to the entryway, with minutes to spare I asked
the steward to take good care of him. "He's eighty years old,"
I said.

"Seventy-nine!" objected my father fiercely.

And the young steward said, "Well, I hope I'm as fit looking
as he is when I reach that age."

And so my father left the United States for the last time. He
liked and admired this country. He felt it had done a lot to
help other countries in the world and that they were not all
suitably grateful. When I was a boy he often told me about
America; he certainly admired American business techniques
and encouraged me to study them—including Gregg shorthand, rather than Pitman, as he said this would be more
useful in the States.

CHAPTER 23

Others' Impressions of PB

As mentioned in the previous chapter, my father spent the month of June, 1977 in Valois, New York, where he granted interviews to many members of Wisdom's Goldenrod Center for Philosophic Studies.

I invited members of this group who wished to contribute their impressions of their meetings with PB to do so for this chapter. They are here presented, along with two from members who met him in Switzerland.

They all asked me to withhold their names.

I put this dialogue with a young girl first because it is direct and to the point. "Out of the mouth of babes . . ." And PB's reply is very revealing.

1) Letter to PB from an eight year-old child:

Lodi, New York
September 20, 1979

Dear PB,

How are you? I'm fine. I am writing this letter right here in my classroom, and we shall begin. Now I want to ask you if you (your intelligent self) can remember your last lives, can you?

I've always wanted to know how you speak to God,

can you tell me or no? If you can, please write back.
Thank you.

Yours truly,

PB replies:

I don't remember my last life, but of the life before I
remember a piece, and that was in the French Revolution. There were three of us who were put in prison and
had to die the next day. But I managed to escape and was
therefore able to set the other two free. We all three got
out of the prison together.

The answer to your second question is I speak to my
Higher Self, as I cannot speak to God. I have to be alone
and keep very quiet. Then the Higher Self may not come
at once, or it may come at once. But I do not speak to it. It
speaks to me.

I send these answers to you as a Christmas present.

2) A second account:

Having heard about PB for nearly ten years prior to meeting
him, and read his books with devout religiosity, my expecta-
tions had constructed an image of a holy man, a gossamer
ethereal being, whose spirituality would hold him above the
ranks of material corporeality, and who might actually take to
the wing at any given moment and vanish before my eyes,
unfettered by the trappings of earthbound existence. To be in
the ranks of the enlightened ones, I thought, was to be barely
"here" at all, or at least only when one chose, which would
naturally be seldom.

Lost in fanciful dreams I looked up as he approached and
caught sight of two very large feet thundering down the path
approaching the building where I was waiting.

Later of course I realized PB did not have large feet at all. He was slight and agile and extremely light of foot! However, in that very first instant I was given a profound lesson whose truth, ten years later, continues to astonish and unfold. Before me was a very human being, one so utterly "present" that my own presence and contact with the moment seemed to be in question, seemed in fact to flash in and out with unsteady awareness. PB was in comparison, more "here," more awake than anyone I had ever seen before. His enlightenment meant a completeness rather than a withdrawal, a thorough mastery and command of the Godly in all its ramifications—down to the most minute detail of living form. He was in touch with a truth in existence, and I was looking elsewhere.

I still vividly recall the last words I was to hear him speak. We had had dinner and he was about to depart. He turned back and looked at us and then quietly said: "Don't misunderstand. The Zen life is the ordinary life."

A third account:

I was twenty-eight years old in 1971 with wife and two children, a full-time post graduate student. The invitation to spend a weekend with PB in Montreux, Switzerland, came to me in London. I seized the opportunity to meet the man whose books had so powerfully affected me since the age of twenty-one.

I arrived in Montreux early in the morning. PB had booked me a room at the Hotel de Paix and I telephoned to say I had arrived. He arranged for me to spend the afternoon with him and sent his secretary to collect me. I purchased a bag of mixed fruits as a gift and had my first meeting with a Sage.

My recollection of my initial reaction is vague, but I do remember the striking quality of his eyes and the overwhelming kindness of his disposition. We walked and talked all afternoon or rather PB talked and I found myself strangely tongue-tied. I remember feeling terribly unworthy of being with such a Being and depressed at the enormous distance I had to travel on the Quest. There were long silences where we sat side by side, and I felt that PB was doing an internal stock-taking of my spiritual state. I felt very ashamed of what he would find and close to tears. He lectured me on not being impatient for progress and stressed that the date of illumination is set by destiny and that impatience only hinders the student. He talked of destiny and freewill and informed me that the freewill we put so much store by in the West is largely illusory and that destiny cloaks itself with the appearance of freewill. We were together for dinner that evening and again the following afternoon and evening.

For much of the weekend I was in a state of emotional tumult as conflicting hopes and anticipations welled up in my breast. I desperately wanted some sort of spiritual experience from him and he recognized this unspoken hope when we said farewell. The clock of destiny must run its course and I had to learn patience and resignation. "At least," he said, "you have had the experience of meeting the man who wrote all those books."

During 1979 I was granted a year's study leave by my university to research material for a book. I planned to spend three months in London gathering the necessary data, and of course I wrote to PB asking if he would see me. To my delight he replied that he would be happy to see me again and invited me to come to Vevey where he then had an apartment. I traveled there and remained for a week.

He seemed much older and frailer than when I had last been with him, but his eyes were still arresting and his mind clear and quick. My first impression of this period, and it is an impression which characterized the entire week, was of a very powerful spiritual force which radiated from him. I had gone with so many questions to ask, and when we had been together for some time and he asked me if I had questions to ask him I found that they no longer seemed important. When I told him he smiled and seemed pleased. As day followed day I found that all I wanted to do was to be near him. If he talked then that was good; if he did not talk then that also was good. My mind did not seem to function very well in his presence and I felt it better just to sit and respond when he felt like speaking.

The highlight of the week came when he asked me to accompany him on a train trip to Geneva on some errand he wanted to do. He had begun fasting several days earlier to remove a small growth under his ear and so he was quite weak. To have a great Being like PB leaning on my arm as we slowly walked about Geneva filled me with pleasure. When his business was done he took me to a tea shop in the old part of the city and we sat there drinking tea for a long time. During this period PB's face began to change before my eyes and as I watched it became the unmistakable visage of Ramana Maharshi. The face did not speak to me but it looked at me with such love that I thought my heart would break. Then the experience passed. I said nothing to PB about it as I thought I must have been hallucinating. But on the train back to Vevey with PB sitting opposite me smiling in meditation, the face of Ramana Maharshi appeared once again. Once again no words were spoken, but I received a look of unutterable love from the face before it became PB's again. The next day I told PB about these experiences and he said they were very good and indicated that Ramana Maharshi would play a major role in my spiritual life and that "You will never be alone again." This comment about Maharshi's involvement in my Quest has been amply borne out since then.

A fourth:

My husband and I were fortunate enough to meet PB on four separate occasions; three day-long meetings in Switzerland during the summer of 1974, and again at Wisdom's Goldenrod in 1977.

At the time of our first visits, PB was seeing very few people, but as we had plans to be in Europe during that period, we decided to ask if he would meet with us. On April 8 of that year, my husband and I sat quietly together and composed a brief letter to Dr Brunton. That night while asleep, I was confronted with two dream images which were remarkably unlike anything I had experienced before. The following morning I recorded both in my journal. The first was a sudden beam of white light which "flew toward me through darkness, and exploded directly in front of my eyes." It was beautiful and startling at the same time. The journal describes it as "similar to watching a snowball hit a windshield from inside a moving car." It was distinctly and clearly the face of PB, and it was amazingly alive and present. He smiled at me, and "multi-colored rays emanated from all around his head." Following each of the images, I awoke with a start, fully alert and trembling with the intensity of those experiences.

For the first meeting, PB welcomed us into his apartment overlooking Montreux. After brief meetings, he politely invited us into his orderly living room which opened onto a small balcony providing a view of the Alps. I was irresistibly and completely drawn to this view. It was lovely, of course, but buildings marred the scene's purity, and I had gazed at more exquisite panoramas of the peaks during our travels in Europe. Why now, upon first meeting a person, was I totally oblivious to social considerations? I simply followed the compelling urge to bask in the atmosphere of that balcony, and stood for a time in the purest peace I had ever known. I was continually aware of PB's presence, and gradually that awareness brought me back to the situation at hand. As if nothing had happened, PB led me back into the apartment and began showing us various objects which adorned the walls and shelves of his home. In retrospect, I understood that he did not lead me or even invite me to step into that glorious state of tranquility. Rather, I was allowed to follow the promptings of an inner call, and it was totally up to me to be sensitive to the moment. Such moments were repeated during the visits with PB, but none held the impact of those first remarkable minutes in his presence.

A fifth:

The day PB first came to Wisdom's Goldenrod Center, there was a large crowd for meditation. The main room had overflowed and people were sitting all around the building—in the hall, in the kitchen. All of us were hoping to see this great man, whose books we'd studied, and who meant so much to our teacher, Anthony Damiani.

Just as meditation ended, I looked up from my seat in the main room, and there was PB. He had come in silently, with the people from the other room crowding, smiling behind him. So simple, so commonplace outwardly, he filled the room with his brilliant serenity. There was no gap, no difference between his body and the rest of the room—his presence filled both in a continuous atmosphere.

The moment I first saw him I knew, without any possibility of doubt, that this goal we aspire and strive for was indeed possible. Here was living proof for mankind that enlightenment was no fantasy but a real thing.

He came in with no fanfare, but absolutely gently and quietly—and changed our lives forever.

During the summer, PB was staying at a nearby home. While he was there, we would route our trips by that corner, in hopes of catching a glimpse of PB—or just to be nearer. Once we had good luck—there he stood, in front of the doorway, framed by the white pillars of the porch, saying goodbye to some visitor. At that moment his radiance seemed so strong that it was physically visible. Later, seeing the halos artists have put around saints, angels and Buddhas, it seemed to me that the basis for the halos must be just that—that impression of a circle of light radiating from a truly holy person.

A sixth:

What does it mean to meet someone of the caliber of Paul Brunton? I was much too young, twenty-four, at the time that I met him, to have more than the slightest inkling of it. Now, in retrospect, I have to ask myself, "What is it about this brief meeting that makes it worth telling?" I find that there are several answers.

For one, PB spoke the way he wrote: nothing was insignificant. His words went to the heart of the matter at hand. And though they may have been directed to an individual seeker with specific needs at a specific time, they were nevertheless universal in their applicability. Each brief message he spoke was like his written messages: concise, simple, direct, and rich with meaning for anyone who cared for it.

Secondly, a little about the way such a man operates was communicated to me, though it was years before I ran across an explanation in his writings of what he meant by the striking statement with which he opened my interview.

Thirdly, although our meeting seems, on the surface of it anyway, to have been quite simple, it was an encounter with a man whose entire life—every gesture and every word—radiated the truth which filled his being and which he had made his own. If I can, in telling of it, convey even the slightest impression of what that was like—or even rekindle in my own mind the memory of it—then it will have been worth the effort.

I met PB in the midst of a torrential downpour. As I stood on the porch of the house where he was staying, waiting to be admitted for my interview, I was not prepared—could have not been prepared—for the quiet, utterly unassuming graciousness of the man who opened the door. His presence was so gentle, so unobtrusive, that it put to shame the nervous remark which I blurted out about the weather. His response, however, was as natural as it was simple: "Well, it can't be helped."

He ushered me into a side room to wait while he finished the interview which preceded mine.

When it came time for my own interview, it was quickly made evident to me that PB worked with a person at a level deeper than that at which their intellect normally troubles them. I was concerned about my lack of specific, prepared questions to ask. But we had barely sat down together when PB rose, walked over to the other side of the room, and uttered a statement which, had I really understood it, should have at least disarmed my anxiety for the remainder of the interview.

He said (and I reproduce his words to the best of my memory): "What happens here today is not really important. What really happens does not take place in time, but it will unfold for you in time because you are in time."

It wasn't until years later, when I came upon a passage in his *Notebooks* (see *Perspectives*, Volume 1 in *The Notebooks*, pp. 354–356) which explains the mysterious way in which an Adept works upon the consciousness of another man, that I really had an idea of the significance of his words.

But for the moment, they had the effect of freeing up my mind to ask some questions which were fairly general, but which nevertheless were of importance to me at the time.

I wanted to know how I could go about finding and following my own individual path on the quest. I was young, and I felt my notions of the quest were general and collective, things I had read in books or heard from others, but not much my own.

PB's answer again was lucid, beautifully simple, yet striking: "Listen to the silence within yourself. Approach it as though it were something to be heard, and it will instruct you."

More words than these, he had no need for.

I also wanted to ask him about a major event which had occurred recently in my life, and see whether he had any insight into its meaning for me. I had been in a serious auto accident in which I was nearly killed . . . but my recovery was now proceeding well, and the experience had had a transformative effect upon my life.

PB asked a couple of questions about it, and then began to talk about karma, and how karma is of two types: there is that which is the result of your own past actions coming back to you, and there is also the karma which is intended to bring the individual more into alignment with the World-Idea. He said this event belonged to the latter type of karma.

He went on to speak about the individual's relationship to the World-Idea, and it was here that another quality of this man became evident: the awe that was inspired in him by the unfathomably grand intelligence which governs the universe. He spoke with wide gestures of the millions and millions of individuals in the world, ". . . and each one of them really is an individual," he said. "And each individual has his own place in the World-Idea."

My interview with PB lasted only fifteen or twenty minutes. Though the few exchanges we had were meaningful, and his words beautiful, it had been made clear from the start that the meeting itself was the essential thing, not any of the specific contents of it. Therefore it was not a surprise to me when he indicated that the meeting should soon come to a close. I had, in fact, asked the only questions that were in me to be asked: nothing else occurred to me later.

PB did, however, have one last message as I got up to leave. I was not, in those days, very well grounded in the common, everyday world of man, and my relationship to it was clouded by the vague and sometimes wild imaginings I had concerning my quest, my fellow seekers, and this strange world of the spirit with which I was acquainted more in imagination than in reality.

His final words to me were, "Remember, amidst all of this *apparent* mysticism, one must retain one's common sense."

It was, of course, his use of that one particular adjective that struck me the most, and provided fuel for much subsequent thought . . . but his simple message of common sense remained with me as well, and was something I came back to often in the following years.

As I left, PB walked to the door with me . . . and I shall always remember the graceful little bow with which he said goodbye, the oriental-style bow with the hands in front, palms together, a gesture which acknowledges, in spite of the imperfections of our egos, the fundamentally spiritual essence in each of us, and reminds us of the delicate spirit of reverence and respect with which we best approach these human—these spiritual—encounters.

A seventh:

PB taught me how to make green tea, which I served him two or three times daily. In the evenings I would also make him a thermos of tea for the sojourn in the wee hours of the night when he would rise and work for a couple of hours. Something was awakened in me by the delicate and conscious manner in which he showed me the tea-making procedures. PB *loved* the perfect tea, with the body full, and the taste subtle. As I followed him through his explanations and motions, I learned something of meditation, grace, and humility. Three or maybe four times daily, I would partake of this beautiful ritual.

In PB's every movement I felt the great reverence he held towards all things—the teapot, the spoon, the counter, the flame. The pouring water from the tap, the relation of one's body to the stove. The listening to the heating water. The waiting. The patience involved was an act of great humility. Stirring the tea in the pot twice at different intervals meant finding that moment in which we are a part of all things. Even the pouring of the tea had a delicacy: the cup, its shape, the liquid and its aroma, were all of one being, with which to be in harmony. Tea-making and serving, and being every moment in PB's presence, showed me that all life, of which we are a part—even the minutest moment—must be approached with respect and reverence, love and consciousness. Every motion we make in this world is a most precious and grace-given experience. Even the most mundane of all actions is filled with Peace. There is no hurry, only consciousness. To carry on one's day with this memory brings appreciation and kindness towards all things. I felt I knew something of the Tao through PB.

An eighth:

Every day in La Tour de Peilz [where PB lived in Switzerland 1980–81], I would get off the bus and walk up the hill to L'Oasis, sometimes a little early, sometimes a little late, for "work" with PB. Sometimes I would linger by the pastry shop half-way up the hill, other times I would jog with my armloads of books, notebooks, and hardware supplies, always hoping to arrive just exactly at 11:00 A.M., the start of our day with PB. Every day I would come in to L'Oasis, catch my breath, get in the tiny elevator, punch #2, ride up to his floor and walk down the hall. Then I would stop and pray. Pray that the archangels and bodhisattvas gathered around PB would protect him and his work from my ego, ignorance, and negativity. I would think of all the light surrounding him, the vast reaches of time behind him and rippling out from his brief stay in history, thinking that it was a hundred years before Islam sprung up out of the footsteps of Mohammed (who only had one true student in his lifetime), and wondering what strange miracle of fate had brought me to that doorway. Then, I would gather my breath and courage, and knock three times (our signal). Immediately the door would swing open and PB was standing there—right there—in front of me, his left hand still on the door handle, his right hand stretched open and inward in sign of welcome, his broad, lopsided smile of greeting: "Please come in."

Many days I would not see him again until lunchtime—he

would retreat down the hall to the living room to continue his work, and I would repair to the study to unpack my bags and begin my work. There was always the rarefied atmosphere of concentration, peace, and light in the room—a strange, unique mixture of library, celestial palace, and the war room of a battle cruiser—intense, demanding pressure combined with steadiness of purpose and pace—and blinding light, at once love, and wisdom, and something more.

Sometimes PB would come sauntering into the study, cock his right leg over the back of a chair and ask, "What's new?" And I would report the stage of the projects he had assigned (once I had thirty-four different tasks on the desk), tell him of gossip from home, tell him of events in the world—whether it was a new train schedule in the local "penny-saver" or the failed rescue mission to Iran. He seemed to expect me to know of these things—and to know what was worth taking his time and attention. It was very difficult to waste time with PB: everything fell into place, or—with painful clarity—fell out of place. Some issues and problems he met with a cold stare; the words, born of anxiety, eagerness, unconsciousness would hang clumsily in the air waiting for order to re-establish itself. Other facts or puzzles would catch his full attention—some dissolved with a quiet word or the shake of his head, and some, some would take us on frightening journeys of discourse and action until the matter was safely and firmly put to rest. He never repeated himself; once a problem was engaged all else stopped until it was solved, permanently solved. Second thoughts were not allowed; they were a waste of time. When a decision was made, the action was engaged, there was no turning back. Even when a better solution later presented itself, PB would reject the issue—if it came up again it would have to wait its time and place.

It was as though each problem, each task had its proper time and priority—PB knew when that was, and would devote his attention and energy to that one thing alone; then when he had done what he could do, or think of doing, he would stop—even if he knew that a compromise had to be taken—but the magic wisdom of knowing when to start, how long to look, and when to push, or when to give up!

So each day passed, some in silence, most filled with conversation during lunch, tea, *moxa* treatments, the moments after sundown. Sometimes there were jokes, sometimes absolutely minute household problems—like matching the right scotch tape dispenser with the right kind of scotch tape (clear in the green ceramic one; cloudy in the old red plastic one; the old yellowed tape in the plastic box the clear one came in)— sometimes anecdotes of Sadat, Subud, PB's younger days, and sometimes spiritual discourse, occult histories, metaphysical queries, or even personal advice. And the daily busyness continued at its curious breakneck, silent steady pace, lasting until 11:00 at night, when my wife and I had to race down the rainy cold hill to catch the last bus back to our little room in the old hotel.

And each night before parting, we would pack our things— taking work for the early morning hours—and then come into the living room to say goodnight. PB would rise, and come towards us; usually he would stop in the middle of his yin-yang carpet, a few feet away from us; he would look at us and smile, and fold his hands together in the Hindu gesture of *namaste*. We did the same, often caught by a wave of love, of sadness, of indescribable life-bonding reverence, I would want to cry, yet crying seemed too physical a thing for the presence before us—and PB would thank us, pausing to pick a phrase, or word, or chant that seemed to capture the quality of the day, and of our moment with him—Namaste; Tien; Om Shanti, Shanti, Shanti; Peace; Good-bye; Good-night; Godspeed.

A ninth:

PB was unusually frail. He was very old when I met him. During the interview we actually said very little—he would smile his odd little smile and then lapse back into silence. He was reading a deep layer of my being, and seemed to know my past, present and future. I was keeping my mind free of thought, but at one point I said mentally, "I'm very glad you came to the Center" or something of that nature, and he flinched! I apologized (mentally) and said that I wouldn't do that again.

At the very end of the interview he told me that music would bring me very close to what I was seeking, but that there was another step. Then he said I should not meditate too much, but some every day. He smiled at me, shook his finger and said quietly, "Now don't forget . . ." I saw pink lights for months after the meeting. I think that I could honestly say that he changed my entire life in the space of forty-five minutes. The details are too personal to record, but yes, I could honestly say that.

A tenth:

In late May 1973 my husband and I visited PB in Montreux, Switzerland with our 2½ year old son. D behaved as many 2½ year olds do—like an untrained puppy. He was extremely excited, a little belligerent, and demanded the undivided attention of everyone. In the beginning of our three-day visit, PB observed D without much involvement with him.

We were often embarrassed by D's behaviour, wishing we could calm him down, but being with a sage made his already energetic nature wild.

In the evenings, when D was asleep or with a babysitter, PB would offer us advice on raising children. About being a parent, he said, "Nature uses you as an instrument of love for the child." He said that the parent must remain detached and keep a delicate balance between the duties to the child and duties to oneself. Also, he advised that the balance between spoiling and disciplining a child must be found, although it is different for each child. But he stressed the importance of teaching a child discipline, because if a parent doesn't teach this, then the world will teach it later in a much more painful way. "It's easier to nip evil in the bud." He said that although discipline is important, hitting or spanking is not the best way. "You must praise the good things a child does."

On the afternoon of the second day we walked to the park along Lac Leman so that D could play outside. PB was relating to D a little more and took him over to see a trained parrot which he thought the child would like. We also had tea in a lovely Moroccan tea house. D was growing calmer, partly because he was finally getting what he had been demanding—PB's attention.

On the last afternoon of our visit, PB was very sweet and attentive to D, playing with him and entertaining him. They played together with Legos which someone had given PB. After lunch, D stood at PB's knee, looked him in the eye and said, "I love you." We had never heard him say this to anyone other than us. PB looked bemused.

D repeated, "You know what, I love you." PB smiled and said, "You must love my beard." Then D reached up and touched PB's beard and caressed him. It was a sweet, touching moment. A little later when we left, PB looked into D's eyes and asked to shake his hand. They shook hands seriously—the Sage and the little boy.

That night D stayed with a babysitter while my husband and I again saw PB, but the last thing PB spoke of was child rearing. He said that D's obstinacy comes from a previous life and might be a good trait on the path. He also said that children must have religious education. It is best given at home, but it should be given intelligently and without superstition so that a child doesn't have to unlearn things. He said that it would be unusual if D weren't a quester since he was born to us. "A quester looks for a family of questers to be born into, so far as he has free will." Again he stressed that we should encourage his positive qualities with praise and have patience.

The next day we all awoke exhausted. D was particularly grumpy, but when we took him to the park, he found some Swiss children to play with and cheered up. When we went into town, he chased after a small old man in a black beret who looked just like PB from the back. We then returned to the Moroccan tea house for afternoon tea. We sat outside, but D needed to use the bathroom inside. His father took him, but on the way back got absorbed in the beautiful artistic tiles that were everywhere. The child ran off, and his father followed him, keeping his eyes on D's little body. D purposefully went toward a certain spot in the restaurant and then stopped. His father stopped behind him and looked up, and there was PB. Feeling that they had invaded PB's privacy, the little boy was coaxed away. A few moments later PB left the tea house, and we all got a last celestial glimpse of him.

Six months later some friends visited PB and came back with a present for D from PB—the little Lego blocks that they had played with together. During the last hours of our visit with PB, I expressed sadness that D was young and would forget his meeting with the Sage. PB said, "He won't forget," and, of course, he was right. D's first memory is that of sitting at the feet of the Sage playing with the Lego blocks.

CHAPTER 24

Vignettes

There are so many memories, many of them too short to be developed but each reminiscent of a happy time, the happy years which I thought would just go on forever. As some of these memories parade across my mind I feel them worth sharing with you and have labeled them *vignettes*.

* * * * *

Once PB explained to me the true meaning of "Goodbye." It means "God be with you," he said.

My father often sent mental "presents" to those who had faith in him and regarded him as their spiritual guide. At the end of his meditations he would visualize certain of his followers and hold them up to the light. (He once told me it was not exactly a white light, but more of a light bluish white light.)

He told me that sooner or later this mental remembrance would enter their consciousness and enable them to go deeper in their own meditation. He once wrote me that being his birthday he was reversing the usual custom and sending me a mental message as a gift! "It will be fourth dimensional so it may or may not come through into the conscious mentality straightway. But it will soon do so anyway," he explained.

* * * * *

One time PB and I were spending the day in the country north of New York City. As noon approached we started looking for a restaurant to have lunch. We were pleasantly surprised to discover an attractive French restaurant. A waitress seated us and then the host approached our table with the menu. I explained that we were vegetarians and asked if he could prepare a vegetable plate for us. Whereupon his face fell and dourly he stated, "A French restaurant is no place for vegetarians!" And he stalked away. But eventually the waitress did bring us our vegetable plates and we managed quite well.

As we were driving away my father told me that when the restaurant owner had made his rude remark, he had heard and felt it reverberating forcefully like a spiral into the atmosphere. And he knew immediately what the result would be, that in some years to come the owner would be afflicted increasingly with stomach pains. He would try various remedies until eventually he would be informed by medical authorities that he had to give up meat-eating! And at that time his memory would flash back to the old gentleman with the white beard who came to his restaurant as a vegetarian.

My father carefully explained that this was in no way his own doing. In no way had he cast a spell over the unfortunate man; but it was the inevitable automatic result of the man's karma incurred with his insult to a spiritually advanced person. Such actions and reactions dovetail, explained PB, quite independently of the persons involved. It is a learning experience whereby the sufferer is educated directly.

We were not always so unlucky in our choice of restaurant. At Lux, for instance, the modest *trattoria* we discovered on our first day in Turin, Italy, the situation was much better. Although there were no vegetarian dishes listed on the menu the *patrone* said he would make something especially for us— and he did. It was so delicious that we went back the next day; again we were treated to a tasty pasta meal, but quite different from the one of the previous day. The chef invited us to return, and so we did for each day of our sojourn! Each day the chef found it an agreeable challenge to prepare a different vegetarian meal for us. What a splendidly positive attitude! And what a difference in each case the owner's attitude made, not only to our enjoyment of the meal but to his own karma.

* * * * *

I used to visit my father two or three times a year for about a week each time. It became a tradition that on the first evening I would ask him, "Are we going to have a treat during my visit?"

And he would invariably answer, "All right, how about tomorrow night?"

We both knew we were referring to a curried dinner. My father was outstanding at preparing a delicious curried vegetable meal. They say everyone carries memories of their mother's cooking and that no one cooks like their mother, but I have never tasted curried vegetables anywhere in India or the West as tasty as my father made them.

* * * * *

Meals were a time of relaxation for my father. He often liked to reminisce about his earlier days and people he had known. But sometimes he would adopt a more serious tone. For instance, one day he discoursed on the age-old Hindu controversy of *Atman* versus non-*Atman*. He would give both points of view and end without arriving at a judgement. It was as though he was thinking out loud—which possibly he was.

* * * * *

Here I am driving from Dayton to Chicago in 1987 and memory takes me back to 1952 when I made the trip overnight in my 1949 Studebaker. The journey took much longer then because there were not the superhighways of today and my car cruised at about 40 miles per hour instead of 70. I had gone on the spur of the moment to visit my father whom I knew was staying at the Edgewater Beach Club on the shores of Lake Michigan just outside Chicago. I reached there at about

9:00 A.M. only to discover that my father had checked out and moved on the day before, leaving no forwarding address! To add to my frustration, my car developed engine trouble and the local dealer would not undertake repairs without payment in advance and would not accept a check on my out-of-town bank.

Eventually we resolved the matter with a telephone call to my Dayton bank, which fortunately was one of my agency's clients, and my check was accepted. But I drove back to Dayton the next day with my tail between my legs and my heart in my boots. As my father wrote me when he learned of my ill-fated trip, "You should have checked first to see that I was still there by telephoning ahead. Always think before you act!" It was a valuable lesson.

* * * * *

As a schoolboy at grammar school in South London I used to spend Saturdays visiting my father who then (in the mid-1930s) was living in Hampstead, England, the historic borough north of the Thames. This was a great treat for me. It was the period when he was working on the proofs of *A Search in Secret Egypt* and allowed me to help him arrange and sort the photographs he intended to include in the book from among the many he had taken during his visit to Egypt. I remember once he asked me to break my journey on the underground railway at Leicester Square and go to a special Chinese store where they sold mung beans and bring them for inclusion in our salad lunch that day. (Fifty years ago mung beans were somewhat of a rarity in the West, now one finds them in every supermarket!) I felt greatly honored to be entrusted with this assignment.

Among later errands I performed for my father was obtaining refills for his German ballpoint pen when I visited Frankfurt each year for the International Bookfair. Before embarking on any travels I would always write and ask if there were anything I could do for him or get him. And quite often there were little things that allowed me to enjoy the feeling of being of service to him.

* * * * *

When my father was eighty-two he said to me, "I thank God for having given me such a long life."

"Why?" I asked.

"Because it is only on this earthly plane that one can make spiritual progress. Oh, yes, we can have many experiences on the other side, many beautiful experiences, but true spiritual progress can only be made here and that is why we are incarnated until we learn and master the lessons of life."

* * * * *

"Don't expect to have a utopia here on earth," he said. "After all, this earth is populated with imperfect people. It is their desires which draw them back to incarnate time after time. So you can't have a perfect world with imperfect people. Therefore it is best to concentrate on what one can do, namely developing one's own perfection. After all, charity begins at home."

* * * * *

My father was a conservationist long before the term became popular. I used to clean his shoes whenever I visited him and one day grumbled about the old can of caked shoe polish. "Why don't we buy a new one?" I asked. "Yes," he replied. "We will, as soon as that tin is used up!"

Perhaps the ultimate in my father's conservation of materials came in his saving paper kitchen towels after use and spreading them out to dry for later reuse.

Please don't get the wrong idea, my father was not stingy by any means. Far from it, he was extremely generous. But he was not wasteful. It was not the financial aspect which concerned him; rather he just did not believe in wasting anything.

And he drilled the same way of life into me. I still will walk a few blocks to save a nickel but equally go out of my way to help a friend in need.

* * * * *

My father was fascinated by trends in razors and pens. He always kept up with the latest developments in both. I well remember his becoming intrigued by a clockwork razor back in 1947. One wound the handle to produce an oscillating blade effect. Whenever a new model or shaving technique came on the market he would be among the first to experiment with it. Indeed his notebooks include instructions on shaving techniques! Pens of all kinds also interested him. He loved nothing better than to browse in a stationer's shop. He would examine with interest any new model of pen. After all, to a writer these were then tools-of-the-trade.

* * * * *

After my father had initiated me into the Short Path in 1956 out at Montauk, New York, he impressed upon me the importance and value of practicing the remembrance exercise during the frenetic pace of busy office routine. One way, he said, was to draw seeming *doodles* that would have a specific spiritual meaning for me. For instance he suggested a five-pointed star or a circle radiating spokes to signify the sun. "Change them frequently," he advised, "so you do not take them for granted and become oblivious to them."

These doodles were drawn by PB as examples to use for remembrance:

"How about writing down words, such as 'Overself,' etc." I asked him.

"Only if you are sure that people sitting across from your desk cannot read your writing upside down!" he replied.

* * * * *

During one of the holidays on which my father took me when I was young, perhaps eight or nine years of age, he took me to a funfair and accompanied me on a miniature toy car ride. So here was this highly developed philosopher cavorting around the rink, grasping a little boy in his lap and bumping into other cars willy-nilly. Whether my father actually enjoyed this or not, I rather question; but he felt it part of his parental duties to amuse a small boy and so he did.

Sometimes he would come to visit my mother and step-father and take me out for an evening. I was always keen to go to the movies and although, as I came to realize in later life, he would have preferred a quiet evening in our home, nevertheless he always acceded to my wishes and took me wherever I wished to go.

Even many years later when I was twenty-four and had been with him for some months in America he had my future very much on his mind and at the right time made an appropriate business connection suitable for me to get started in the world. Again he felt this part of his parental duty and he would conscientiously discharge this duty fully.

Even when we were separated during the war he would still write me regularly with letters of advice suitable to my circumstances. Some extracts from these letters are given separately in Chapter 7—not for what they say about me, but for what they reveal about their writer at that time and his ongoing concern throughout those difficult years.

* * * * *

My father grew strikingly more handsome as he became older. He had grown his moustache while in India in 1932 and he thereafter kept it. And in 1952 he added a small goatee which enhanced his appearance. In his seventies he adopted the "Mao" style of moustache with the down-turned ends. He liked this very much and asked me why I too did not adopt it.

"Well, it's not regarded with much favor in the conservative upper-echelons of the business world," I replied.

"Then I'm glad I'm not a businessman and can do what I like!" he laughed.

With advancing years his features appeared to become more aquiline and his skin so fine as to be almost transparent. He had a most distinguished-looking appearance.

Once, in the mid-1960s, we were riding together on a tram in Lugano when a lady seated opposite became quite smitten by his looks. Bending over to me, she asked in Italian if he were my father.

"Si, signora," I answered.

"Bella! Bella!" she remarked approvingly.

And throughout this interchange I could sense my father beaming with pleasure!

* * * * *

PB was always self-conscious of his lack of height. He mentioned to me he felt that taller men had an advantage physically when they entered a room. I reminded him of Napoleon's lack of physical stature—and he smiled!

Once in examining a photograph of himself he remarked to me that his mouth always came out as a "gash" as he felt it was too thin.

* * * * *

My father refrained from going to barber shops for haircuts. He was too sensitive to the odors and vibrations of strange barbers. For thirty-five years he asked me to cut his hair during my stays with him. His hair was very fine which no doubt accounted for his early baldness in his twenties. (A trait which I inherited.) I took pride in cutting it with the scissors and shaving his neck with an electric razor. In fact it was a loving experience to hold his head in my hands and wait upon him.

* * * * *

Sunset was not only a favorite time of day for my father but was also of particular significance. Once when we were vacationing in Portugal and staying at the town of Lagos, he said he would like to find a clear site from which to observe the sunset. It struck me that the airport might be suitable, and so we drove out there and watched the setting sun from the observation deck.

As we did so PB remarked: "The Egyptians knew what they were doing when they worshipped the sun, it is the closest thing we have to visualizing the Creator."

He then indoctrinated me into the sunset and sunrise meditations. These are listed among the exercises he gives in *The Wisdom of the Overself*, Chapter XIV.

Most importantly, he said, "Try to hold that last disappearing ray of the sun as it goes down over the horizon. Concentrate on it just as one does on the disappearing sound of *Om* in meditation."

* * * * *

Oh, so many walks over the years with my father! He enjoyed strolling and most of all in a park or wood where he could enjoy the vibration of Nature. He pointed out that we need the greenery as a change of pace to refresh our eyes and to inhale its oxygen-giving properties. Often he would reminisce or open up a discourse on current world affairs or open a topic of spiritual import. Yes, we walked in all of London's parks and commons, and across Hampstead Heath (which was his favorite)—and in many other parks throughout Europe. In France, Italy, Spain, Portugal, Germany and Switzerland. Perhaps best of all he liked walking the length of the flower gardens along the lake at Montreux. They were beautifully decorated with various blooming plants and flowers, even magnolias, palms and fig trees. In fact the local inhabitants had erected a monument to the chief gardener! We often strolled along here admiring the open view of Lake Geneva framed by the Alps on both sides.

I can see him now, hands clasped behind his back as was his wont, leisurely perambulating—and for some reason I am reminded of the walk of Charlie Chaplin's little tramp who brought to laughter what my father brought to philosophy. They were both symbols in their own way. Indeed my father admired Chaplin's art and devoted a whole chapter to it in his book *A Hermit In The Himalayas*.

* * * * *

Among my father's multitudinous notes are many dealing with mundanely practical details of life. These probably will never be published in book form as they are unlikely to appeal to a large audience. Yet he often considered writing such a book. Its model would have been *How to Live Twenty-Four Hours a Day* by Arnold Bennett, whose writing style he admired. One afternoon he and I were having tea at the Tres Coronnes Hotel in Vevey, and happened to browse through their shelves of English language books in the library. There we discovered a copy of Bennett's book, and my father recommended it to me. Afterwards I bought a copy which I later gave to him and which he kept.

He gave me much practical advice over the years, some of which does not seem to be in his notes. For instance, while visiting him in Auckland, New Zealand, in 1962 (where I stayed three weeks with him) he told me that the toxins in the body follow the law of gravity and accumulate in the feet. And they gradually work their way through the surface of the skin. He said the way to get rid of them was to soak one's feet for twenty minutes in warm water liberally laced with epsom salts. He said this would eat away at the toxins. But, as mentioned earlier, he cautioned about the need to rinse the feet in clear water afterwards; otherwise the salts would keep eating away, he warned! In fact he also recommended a monthly bath immersing the whole body in the mixture of warm water with epsom salts. These practices do indeed leave one with a feeling of extreme cleanliness and freshness—and I'm surprised that the practice is not more widely known.

While I was in my twenties PB suspected that I had a sluggish liver and suggested that the best cure for this condition was to stimulate the liver each morning by drinking a glass of hot water. "In fact," he said, "why don't you make the water more palatable by putting a tea bag in it—and having a cup of tea!" I have followed his advice for more than forty years in this matter and it has become an ingrained habit—just as I discovered it was with PB himself.

My father gave me much practical advice in everyday living. For example, whether it was because of his ingrained efficiency or because of his thoughtfulness for others, PB taught me to put the town in capital letters when addressing an envelope and to underscore it, "Why not make it easy for the postman!" And this, and many other tips he taught me, have become second nature.

* * * * *

At the age of fourteen, on one of the Saturdays spent with my father when we used to have what I realize now were discussions on spiritual subjects (although they seemed very natural to me at the time) I said to PB that I felt uneasy about losing my individuality upon achieving *Nirvana* (quite a presumptuous statement coming from a fourteen year-old!) But PB accepted my statement at face value and went on to explain that we do not completely lose all sense of individuality. We continue to exist but to exist *in* and surrounded by and as part of the greater Whole. He gave me the illustration of a wave on the lake. "Which is the wave and which is the lake?" he asked. "What is the difference between them? You have hundreds of waves upon even a small lake."

"A wave is the ocean expressing as a wave. It has form and shape and movement. It has an identity and a uniqueness, but is no more no less than the ocean. It is not even limited to a particular segment of ocean. It is a movement within the ocean, a projection of the ocean, which at the same time moves on and through the ocean. When a wave crashes on the shore, where is the ocean water that formed the first swell? Right back there in the deeps where it always was."

* * * * *

In his letters to me during the war, my father talked about our working together after the war, a time when I would be able to help him, and he talked about our working together on his proposed magazine.

Well, it did come about of course—as mentioned earlier— that I spent almost a year with him following my arrival in the US in May 1947. And I helped him in a secretarial and house- hold capacity. But the following spring he helped me obtain the training position in the Midwest advertising agency where I was to spend five years before taking up a career in book publishing.

In later years it occurred to me to ask PB whether I had failed him, whether I had let him down in some way by pursuing a career of my own rather than staying with him and serving as his secretary. Was I weighed in the balance and found wanting?

"No, not at all! I never even thought such a thing," he replied. When I pressed him on the matter he said, "No, I gave up my plans for a postwar magazine and anyway you did serve with me for some time. That was more to enable me to give you a sound spiritual grounding but I was also able to impart some practical worldly training as well which has served you in good stead. Thus I fulfilled my duty to you." (As I write these lines and recall his words vividly I wish I had questioned him further about this duty of his in our relation- ship. But there you are. I did not and the time has gone.)

"Anyway," he continued, "you did serve as my mail secretary for many years. You emptied the mailbox regularly and sorted through the mail and answered what you could and handled matters for me. So that part has been fulfilled."

And of course he was correct. I acted as his mail secretary and forwarding agent until he finally left America to settle permanently in Switzerland. (At that point he arranged for his mail address for readers to be care of Grindlays Bank at 16 St James's Square in London. He told me afterwards, somewhat ruefully, that he regretted this as the word "bank" gave people the impression that he was a wealthy person—which he was not!)

* * * * *

My father had a charming way of instructing me. When he wanted to make a point he would often phrase it in the first person singular. We were walking along a street in Dayton, Ohio, in 1950 and he volunteered, "Whenever I am out walking and find a woman approaching me in the opposite direction, I deliberately look away from her for I do not want her to feel 'Oh, dear, here's another one of those men ogling me and looking at my breasts.' Besides," he continued, "at your younger age it will help you restrain any difficult impulses! So you are doing yourself a good turn as well as the woman."

* * * * *

PB always lived unostentatiously in simple surroundings. He preferred small apartments in blocks of flats where he would be less likely to draw attention to himself than if he were in a separate house in the suburbs. He kept aloof from his neighbors and politely evaded social invitations.

He told me once that his horoscope foretold ill luck with living quarters and he was never able to stay much longer than a year without problems arising which would force him to move.

At his last residence in La Tour de Peilz, Switzerland, the

teenage son of his neighbors would come home from school about 3:00 P.M. each day and play loud hard-rock music which penetrated the walls of PB's apartment. My father adjusted himself to the situation by going out at that time for a couple of hours to attend to his shopping or walking exercise—and thereby avoiding the intrusion of the loud music.

As we returned to his flat one evening he commented to me that he always enjoyed returning to his "humble abode" after being out; he felt it cozy and in the winter months warm and inviting. I suspect it was also a haven from the impact of the materialistic vibrations of the outside world.

* * * * *

In February 1988 I had the pleasure of meeting Walter Starcke who was the keynote speaker at the Spiritual Advisory Council's winter conference in Orlando, Florida. It transpired that Walter was not only an avid reader of my father's books, but had actually met him once in person. Walter told me that it was my father's works which had introduced him to the higher thought. One day when he was a struggling young actor on Broadway, Walter had wandered into the Gotham Bookmart, the famous bookstore for occult books in Manhattan, and the owner suggested he read Paul Brunton's *The Quest of the Overself*. Walter did so, and then read the rest of PB's books avidly. Walter went on to become a famous stage director of such hits as *Bell, Book and Candle, I Am a Camera*, and many others. He later also became a close friend and follower of Joel Goldsmith, author of *The Infinite Way* and *The Art of Meditation*. Goldsmith was highly regarded by my father and met with him several times.

I quote from a letter dated January 8, 1987, from Walter Starcke to Reverend Paul V. Johnson, President of the Spiritual Advisory Council:

> What I'm really writing you about is my joy at the re-
> surgence of Paul Brunton. He was a friend of Joel's and
> spent some time in Hawaii with him. One time in New York

City about 1956, Joel asked me to join them for lunch and
meditation. The three of us meditated in Joel's suite at the
Hotel Plaza, went to lunch, and spent the afternoon meditating on and off.

Brunton was a true gentle man. His presence was gentle
and his spirit was gentle, not self-effacing, but certainly
accepting without any need to project himself into the situation.

* * * * *

Once my father and I were on a bus in New York City when
for some reason I reminded him that in my horoscope (which
he had drawn at the time of my birth and which had proven
remarkably accurate in all its details) he had forecast that I
would be "liable to broken bones through an accident."

Immediately he said, "Put that thought out of your mind
completely. Erase it, do not encourage it."

He went on to explain that what we think about we tend to
attract into our lives, especially if we hold it long enough and
strongly enough.

"What about karma?" I asked. "If it's meant to be will it not
happen?"

"Not necessarily," he replied. "Karma can be, and often is,
modified or even changed completely. I don't mean that we
escape the effects of the karma we have earned, but it can be
balanced against other karma and in many cases dissolved, or
it may come about in a different form. But never encourage
your so-called bad karma, leave it up to the powers that be,
they know better than you."

"But . . ." I argued.

"Your natal horoscope shows the situation of your character
and personality at the time of your birth," my father continued. "But that was more than fifty years ago. In the mean-
time it's reasonable to expect you have changed during those
fifty years, hopefully for the better, and therefore it might not
be necessary for some of the bad karma you brought into this
life with you to occur. Karma is not punishment, as many

people believe, it is education, an educative process. That is its purpose. If you no longer need that particular lesson to be hammered into you, then that particular piece of karma would not come about in exactly that way; it would be greatly modified or could be negated altogether by another piece of good karma which you have built up and balanced against it. So don't take these too seriously. In any case, astrology is not an exact science by any means and if a man has enough strength of character he could tear up his horoscope and forge his own destiny. In your case you came into this world with a great deal of karmic obligations which you are being given the opportunity to deal with in this lifetime, rather than work them out over a number of lives. And because of your close association with me both the good and the bad have been stirred to the surface for you to become aware of and to deal with. So even though my astrological predications for you were accurate at the time of your birth, they are no longer necessarily so. In fact I doubt if they would be."

He went on to explain that many people who came into contact with him found their karma being speeded up. He said he seemed to be a (largely undeliberate) catalytic agent in stirring up their karma and bringing it to the surface, both good and bad. He said that many people did not appreciate the bad karma—even though, he pointed out, it was to their benefit to know about it, to be in a position to deal with it, and to have it done with once and for all rather than postponed to some future date. Otherwise they would be completely unaware of this so-called bad under the surface of their consciousness so he was really doing them a favor by drawing it to their attention! (For those who wish to know more about my father's ideas on karma, the reader is directed to Volume 6 in *The Notebooks of Paul Brunton* series.)

* * * * *

My father's attention to detail was boundless. He studied the instructions for appliances carefully, and rather than trust memory committed them to paper. I have several notebooks of his filled with instructions for using various dictating machines, electric shavers, etc., etc.

Having typed several of those original paragraphs for his notes, they remain in my memory—and indeed I follow them today. For example, he once told me that it is a good idea, when using an electric shaver, to go over one's face once and then turn off the machine for a few minutes before completing the shave a second time. He explained that by not running the shaver too long and by giving it a rest, its life would be prolonged. Whether this is so or not, I do not know, but I do follow the practice automatically.

* * * * *

Often when traveling with my father in foreign countries, I rented a car for us. I did the driving while my father lay prone on the back seat—often scribbling notes or embarking upon a conversation. He did not drive himself. The only occasion I have heard of his taking the wheel was once in California when he was driving with Dan Franz. Dan later told me that it was a hair-raising experience for him as my father took the corners at speed. In fact, Dan claimed PB must have used second sight going around those corners!

* * * * *

Often I find myself walking behind someone on the street who reminds me of my father. They will be dressed simi-larly—complete to the beret and blue raincoat—and as I hasten to overtake them from the side I will have a glimpse of a grey goatee beard, just like PB's. But of course a few more steps and I see it is not him. How could it be? So I must quiet my heart from thumping.

* * * * *

Those who knew my father only in his last ten years of life saw only one side of him.

The photograph used on the jackets of the cloth-bound editions of *The Notebooks of Paul Brunton*, taken in Lugano by my good friend Dr Arthur Broekhuysen, portrays a dignified elderly gentleman. In fact, if you were to send to central casting for a photograph of a philosopher, this is what you would get. And indeed this was the elder PB in his final years.

But there was another PB. I remember him also as he was in his thirties and forties—a veritable dynamo of energy.

The drawing by Dr Gottfried Meyer which I used on the book jacket of *Essays on the Quest* shows him at what I consider his prime, in his fifties. Note the lofty intellectual forehead, the piercing but compassionate eyes, the mouth slightly wrinkled into a smile, and the determined chin behind his goatee.

* * * * *

Every now and then PB comes into the periphery of my eye and I espy him—but the moment I turn he is gone.

* * * * *

The first chapter of this biographical reminiscence relates my father's illumination in his own words. But in addition, the following which he told me in July 1979 and which I wrote down word for word may be worthy of note:

> My own final illumination happened in 1963. There was this bomblike explosion of consciousness, as if my head had split open. It happened during the night in a state between sleeping and waking, and led to a deepening of the stillness: there was no need to meditate. The verse in the *Bhagavad Gita* which mentions that to the Knower the day is as night and the night is as day became literally true, and remains so. It came of itself and I realized that the Divine had always been with me and in me.

* * * * *

My father had a great love for beauty. He used to save ʼrthday cards, greeting cards, Christmas cards, even calendars long after they were out of date—if the illustration appealed to his esthetic sense.

* * * * *

There was considerable confusion among people regarding my father's birth date. He deliberately fostered an erroneous date because he did not wish to have people drawing up astrological charts of him all over the world! The official birth date was given as November 27, 1898 . . . but the true date was October 21, 1898, as he himself confirmed to me in a letter dated October 7, 1969.

* * * * *

My father believed in the importance of formal education even though he felt it did not go far enough by any means. He made sure that in my late teens I was well immersed in Kant, Descartes, Hume, Locke, Berkeley, Mill, *et al.* in my academic philosophy studies. He stressed the importance of having a good background in these formal philosophic tenets in order to more fully comprehend the principles which he would present later. As PB was away from England during those years I was unable to discuss my studies with him directly. When we did meet up again after the war he questioned me on them thoroughly, especially Emmanuel Kant's *The Critique of Pure Reason* for which he had high regard although he felt Kant had stopped short of making the final leap into mentalism.

* * * * *

In 1965 I invited my father to come to America with me on the maiden voyage of the new Italian liner the *Rafaello*. I knew he liked traveling by sea and I felt the rest and relaxation would benefit him. He agreed and I made the bookings.

In July I flew to Nice, France, where I was met by PB and Dr Arthur Broekhuysen at the airport. (I should here mention that Arthur was and is a longtime student of my father. He had written PB from his own native Holland care of the British publishers and was delighted to receive a reply that PB planned to visit the Netherlands soon and would be pleased to grant an interview. In due course, following the interview, PB asked Arthur whether he would be willing to help in a secretarial capacity, making his hotel and travel arrangements, etc.—and Arthur readily agreed. Thus started a thirty-five year close association. And it is interesting to note that Arthur Broekhuysen, who is well versed in my father's philosophy, has also started to write articles reflecting it in the years since PB's passing.) With Arthur Broekhuysen, as with myself, PB would often forward reader letters for him to reply to and if it seemed indicated, to meet with them and discuss PB's philosophy. Both of us felt it a great honor to be so entrusted.

The three of us spent a few days in Nice, staying at the same modest hotel and then I rented a car and we drove along the French Corniche through the Riviera and crossed the Italian border at San Remo, where we stopped for lunch. We arrived in Genoa late that evening where we obtained rooms at the Hotel Victoria, notable in my memory for the lengthy flights of stairs we had to climb from the street to the reception lobby! After a few days Arthur left us to return to The Hague and PB and I embarked on the *Rafaello*. We had a marvelous eight days together without any outside pressure or interruptions. We frequented the ship's library and enjoyed watching its movies at night—including *Lawrence of Arabia* dubbed in Italian! I told the *maitre d' hôtel* we were vegetarians and this was no problem with the wide variety of Italian pastas on the menu. A lovely voyage—can it really be almost a quarter of a century ago?

* * * * *

PB was in Europe in 1975 when I was admitted to a hospital in New York with a heart attack. But he was promptly informed and I'm sure his thoughts were with me during the ~nth in which I hovered between life and death. A few months later when I had recovered well enough to visit Europe and discuss the situation with him, he explained it thusly:

> The World-Mind was saying to you that you have been very successful in a worldly sense with your life, but what are you going to do with the rest of it now that you are fifty-two years old? Especially, what are you going to do in the spiritual sense? You were given the choice and you agreed to devote yourself fully to the spiritual life which is why you pulled through and lived.

I also told him about the clairvoyant experience resulting from the heart attack which showed the world to me in a different light. Indeed it was rather frightening as I felt I was not ready for it. PB confirmed the accuracy of my vision and said, "Yes, it will fade in time but the memory of it will always be with you."

* * * * *

As you prepare yourself for sleep after finishing your mental exercises, recommended my father, imagine yourself being rocked to sleep in the arms of your Higher Self, just like a baby in its mother's arms, and feel its loving support and protection.

* * * * *

"Most questers feel that self-illumination is far off, a goal to be reached in some future life. But you can achieve it in this same lifetime IF you desire it strongly enough. After all, you ARE going to attain it someday, why not make up your mind it will be sooner rather than later? Go all out for it! And then even if you don't succeed in this life, the results of your hard work will show in the next life so it will still be worthwhile."
—PB to the author in 1977

* * * * *

One day when Arthur Broekhuysen and I were visiting PB in Montreux at the same time, the three of us took an excursion up to the village of Caux higher up in the hills. Here we discovered the old headquarters of the Moral Rearmament Movement, founded by Frank Buchman before World War II. The large building is now used for conferences by many international groups. At the time of our visit people were checking in for a conference of some kind. We wandered around and then my father said, "Let's find somewhere quiet where we can meditate." So we found an empty chamber, went in, sat on three of the chairs along the walls, closed our eyes, and went into meditation. Sometime later I was aware of the door opening and closing several times; eventually I opened my eyes to find a dozen people in the room with us all sitting quietly and presumably meditating. Apparently they thought it was on the schedule of activities! My father afterwards said we did them a good turn!

* * * * *

My father and I often discussed the international outlook and the possibility of another war. He often expressed his thought that mankind had gone too far in thinking thoughts of hatred and ill will toward one another and that this had to materialize on the physical plane. Yet when we last discussed the situation in February 1981 he told me he felt the odds had improved to fifty-fifty.

As of this writing in late 1988 the odds seem to be improving even further with the *rapprochement* between the USA and the USSR and the peace negotiations being carried on in so many other trouble spots. But PB warned that even if we escape a nuclear Armageddon there are other perils to be confronted. I distinctly remember him saying years ago that we will be sorry about chopping down trees indiscriminately—and this long before the environmentalists woke to the danger of stripping our natural resources.

Later he pointed to other serious dangers confronting our planet—overpopulation, famines, acid rain, deforestation, etc., etc. He explained that all these problems could only be solved by a cooperation between the nations of the earth. Acid rain for instance affects so many countries that all have to combine in tackling it. The effect, he said, will be to force the different nations toward a cooperative society, if not a one-world government. The history of mankind has evolved from the family unit into the tribe into the city-state into the nation into the large power-blocs; no longer can we exist on this tiny planet without joining hands to work out the solutions to these fearsome problems.

* * * * *

My father's first student in England was Hesper LeGallienne Hutchinson. She was the daughter of Richard LeGallienne, the English poet and literary critic, and half-sister of Eva LeGallienne, the famous actress. She was married to Robert Hutchinson, an American novelist. They preferred to live in England and during World War II headed up the American Red Cross there. Hesper was an accomplished poet and I have placed one of her poems, a tribute to my father, at the front of this book.

When I was a young boy my father took me to Robert and Hesper's large country home at Tonbridge Wells. I did not meet them again until 1953 when they were living in a pre-revolutionary manse at West Redding, Connecticut. PB and I drove out to spend a weekend with them and we shared a large double bed in their guest room. I remember thinking how nice it was to feel like a small boy again sleeping in my father's bed!

I liked the Hutchinsons very much and went to see them often. Hesper had a small "Quiet Room" in which she arrayed her oriental *objets d'art*. She reserved this room for meditation and spiritual study. The poem at the front of this biography refers to my father visiting the room with her during our stay.

I was extremely touched when upon her death she left me her Siamese Buddha, which was the centerpiece of the room, together with an ancient Tibetan thangka. These two items are now the centerpieces of my own collection in my own meditation gallery!

CHAPTER 25

Health Problems in Later Years

My father believed in taking good care of the body ". . . as it is the instrument through which we have to function." He was careful in his diet and by and large took very good care of himself. But the years he spent in India were deleterious to his health and he consequently suffered from fevers and malaria quite often. In 1953 when I was staying with him in Connecticut he was recovering from a debilitating illness known as sprue which he had contracted in the tropics. But once again, using short fasts and mental affirmations, he was able to overcome this malady.

After his death some friends told me that he had suffered a mild stroke in May 1979 and that one doctor had diagnosed a brain tumor; but this diagnosis was contradicted by another physician. My father told me nothing of this at the time; he merely wrote in a letter dated May 17, 1979:

Had to do something for my health, a little trouble, so fasted five days on nothing at all, then added five more days on liquid herb tea. Broke fast six days ago and now on new diet. Perhaps next few months will settle the matter; doctor is puzzled and can't identify.

On August 9, 1979, he wrote:

Yes, I've had health problems this year but the worst one has seemed to have vanished after a ten-day fast. The other

one is of uncertain nature but diet changes may clear it up. I
visited the Rudolf Steiner clinic near Basel to get diagnoses.
Tahini no longer, tea in small quantities only, all liquid
reduced.

I visited my father in October 1979 and he seemed in good
health. I again visited him in the spring of 1980—at which
time he told me he had had hernia and scrotum surgery. He
seemed to be recovering well and was undertaking acupuncture from a Swiss doctor.

It was in a letter dated July 12, 1980 that he congratulated
me on my latest professional accomplishments and wrote,
"You seem to have fresh inspiration with these maturer years,
and a higher level too. Yes, all leading somewhere."

But on November 30, 1980, he wrote:

There have been some changes in my health condition. The
first has been that my memory has weakened so names and
addresses are more quickly forgotten. But they are trouble-
some. For instance one change was a month ago I went to
Lausanne to attend to some matters there, among which
was to pay the rent of the apartment. But when I reached
near the office to pay the money, I could not remember its
exact address. So this caused some problems and I had to
ask the police to help me, which they did. Another difficulty which happened was I have unsteady hands so I had
to give up writing instruments as I could not write a letter.
Also it did not help to use the typewriter. Thirdly I forgot
how to spell properly. My physician is not yet sure what is
wrong. He thinks it may pass away, but if it does not he will
recommend a specialist in neurology to look into the matter. I should like to mention the case of Emerson who
started forgetting when he was eighty years old and he
used go into *samadhis*. I have been going into *samadhis* quite
frequently lately. Once it happened in a restaurant for half
an hour. Meanwhile the doctor is giving me one powerful

medicine and the other is homeopathic. And we have to see what effects these medicines have. I've not been with these medicines one whole month. But I'm managing the household and shopping matters.

On December 7, 1980, my father wrote:

A series of work pressures and new physical problems came together and interrupted what was being prepared for your visit in February. The work concerned foreign edition books (Portuguese version) which is now off in the post until the revisions and the changes which I have sent to Brazil can be dealt with by the publishers either fully or to the extent they are willing to go along with it. The health problems interfered with my sight, making it hazier, and shifted my capacity to formulate words and sentences. My doctor is not quite sure what is the cause. But he is trying out medicines, both allopathic and homeopathic. It may be a case of *dyslexia*. I cannot find this word in the dictionary. This problem occurs mostly in young people who grow out of it. And at times it occurs with some elderly people. Spelling of words is interfered with and made difficult and words are mixed up. Also the hand trembles. Writing is interfered with so I had to give it up and stop writing letters or anything at all. The only way to communicate is by dictation. However a little improvement has begun in the writing. But I must continue to watch and await results. The doctor thought the trouble may pass away but he doesn't know yet.

When I visited my father in February 1981 for a week I was disturbed to find him a changed man. In many ways he seemed the same PB but there were significant changes. He seemed physically frail and slow in his responses. It was difficult for him to tackle many minor chores, such as tying his shoelaces or knotting his tie. Yet he persevered determinedly.

For instance, in all the preceding years when we prepared meals, my father had taken charge and done the actual cooking while I would peel potatoes and prepare vegetables at his direction. But now I suddenly realized our roles were reversed. He was following me around the kitchen and clearly expected me to take the lead. I didn't say anything but this turn of events saddened me.

The visit was a quiet one. We sat most afternoons on a bench by the lake without saying much. Several times when I tried to broach subjects which normally would have been of some interest to my father, he seemed disinterested. But he made a point of taking me around and introducing me to people. He took me to his lawyer and to the crematorium society which he had prepaid to cover expenses of his cremation. As far back as May 1973 PB had discussed what should be done at the time of his death and had dictated to me the outline of an "action" plan. This was later changed and refined over the years. He was very efficient in preparing me for the occasion of his death, especially as matters had to be handled under local Swiss law with which I would not be familiar. It was a big benefit to me when the time finally arrived.

It was unseasonably mild in La Tour de Peilz for that time of year. We had been out shopping and were returning to his apartment, walking up the street with our groceries when my father inquired if I had any plans for retirement in the near future.

"No," I replied, "I'm still very active in my career and feel that I can still continue to make a contribution to improving educational tools in Third World countries. Besides, I don't really know what I would do in retirement."

"I thought you always wanted to write," said PB.

"But I've nothing to write about. One has to have something to say before one settles down to write, surely?" I rejoined.

"Well, you could write about the quest as you have followed

it and lived it in the world. That would be of interest to other questers and you could give them some advice."

"Oh, come on, PB, what advice could I give!" I exclaimed.

"Why not combine your earlier advertising copywriting background with what you know now about the quest and present it to people in simple everyday terms? After all there are enough of us writing at the higher levels of philosophy, what is needed in this age of the common man, of *Kali Yuga*, is to make these basic truths plain not only to the man in the street but indeed to the man in the back street!"

I demurred, but PB reminded me of how he had encouraged me thirty-five years earlier when I was writing articles for an industrial company's house organ to inject a spiritual truth here and there.

"Now you know much more and have experienced much more on the quest and so you can give much more."

How foolish we can be! There I was pleading I had nothing to say and yet a few years later I was burning with the urge to pass on what I knew—both in lectures and in articles and books. I know now it is indeed a spiritual law to pass on what one has learned; otherwise one jams up the flow of truth— one has to pass it on to make room for more truth to enter one's life.

After my return to the United States I checked medical authorities and wrote to my father that their consensus was that he had had a stroke and that this was the cause of the problems with his coordination of hands, arms, speech, spelling, etc. I received a reply from my father in his own (slurred) handwriting stating: "This was a bombshell!"

The letter ended: "Are you able to read my writing, please let me know." And the letter is a testament to the determination of my father to overcome his illness. It must have been painful, requiring a great deal of concentration, to write a two-page letter . . . but he persevered and certainly I could read it.

His last letter to me was dated May 24, 1981, confirming my visit for the following October and in which he wrote:

My doctor said his homeopathic medicines had not succeeded. He wanted to put me on embryos but I would not
accept them although they were the last resort so he tried
me on acupuncture. After three trial treatments I was much
better so shall continue regularly. My handwriting is still a
bit awkward but as you can see I can write a letter which
was not possible earlier. I eat well and feel cheerful. With
peace and affection,

This was the last letter I was to receive from my father. I still
have every letter he ever wrote me from 1939 for the next
forty-two years—and they are very precious to me.

In June 1981 PB spoke on the telephone to a close mutual
friend, Mrs Evangeline Glass. She recorded their conversation and later wrote down his remarks. How beautiful they
are! How inspiring!

I am cheerful on the whole. Trying to adjust to a faulty
body. Inwardly I am having truly wonderful experiences.
Yes, extraordinary things are happening on the inner plane.
I have proof that Divinity is there. We are not left alone—It
is in charge. I have more confirmation now. At times before
it was hard to accept even for me when I looked around at
the evil in the world. But I know, even though things look
the opposite and black from our limited standpoint, it is
Divinity behind it all—from the standpoint of God.
All is well. Man has created his own darkness. I see it all
more clearly now. We are not left alone. It is there. Even if
things look the opposite. He is behind all with a great plan.
We can receive miracles and healing. I see this more clearly
than ever before. On the Higher Plane all is in Divine
Order.

CHAPTER 26

PB's Transition

The fateful day arrived. Saturday, July 25, 1981. I had paint-ers at my home in Nyack, New York, and was supervising their work when the telephone rang in the early afternoon. It was Paul Cash calling from Switzerland.

"You had better sit down, Kenneth," he said.

And he went on to tell me that PB had been hospitalized and was in a coma at a local hospital. I replied that perhaps we should wait until we had more definite information about his condition and I asked Paul to telephone me in the morning with an updated medical report. Then I sat quietly to absorb this bombshell. I knew it would have to come one day but a part of me refused to accept it. It just couldn't be! Yet . . . it was. I felt a vacuum-like power telling me to go immediately to Switzerland that Saturday and not wait another day. I called Paul back and told him I would leave immediately and one way or another arrive there the following morning.

I telephoned Swissair and was able to book the last seat on their evening flight to Geneva. I then shooed the painters out of my house, quickly packed a suitcase and telephoned for a taxi. On the way to JFK airport I stopped at my office and scribbled various notes to my staff before continuing to catch the plane just in time.

I will not attempt to describe my feelings during that long journey. Since I had seen my father five months earlier in

February his letters had been cheerful and upbeat. He was continually writing and although it was evident he could write only with difficulty and laboriously nevertheless his indomitable spirit persevered. I had high hopes for a recovery. After all, eighty-three is not so old these days, and anyway I just expected PB to go on forever, always to be there.

I took the train from Geneva to Vevey, and then a taxi to my father's apartment at 109 Avenue des Alps in the suburb of La Tour de Peilz. Here I was greeted by Paul Cash. He told me how the afternoon before he had been working in the study while my father was in the living room when he heard a noise.

Paul continued: "PB was at work, writing; the stroke came—at least to me—as a surprise. He had been in a cheerful playful mood throughout the day, very light-spirited, and in his fun-to-be-with mood. There was no outward indication at all of what was coming.

"That mood, in fact, was frequently with him through July. He was pleased that progress was being made through the acupuncture treatments. He was eating well, and he generally felt quite cheerful. He worked at writing some every day, applied himself to handling correspondence, and carried on his normal inner work.

"At about 4:00 Saturday afternoon he came out from a short rest in his room. While we had tea, he looked over a couple of letters I had written up for him, and he told me what he wanted to say in a third one. I went into the front office to write that letter and PB went back to work revising some of his original material from about three years ago.

"Shortly after I began the letter, I heard just a few muffled unusual sounds from the other room, and decided just to check in on PB to see if there was anything wrong. He seemed stunned. I asked him if he needed help, and only then did I realize that he couldn't speak. So I took his hands and said that if he wanted an ambulance he should squeeze my hands. He let go at first, but then a few moments later, he seemed to be trying to squeeze, so I went to the telephone and called the hospital.

"In a few minutes the ambulance arrived. They put PB on the stretcher, and he stretched out his left hand to me to stay with him. I took that hand and held it until we arrived at the intensive care unit of the hospital. The peace and calmness did not diminish at any time. In fact, when we arrived at the hospital, everything was so intensely calm that no one at first realized the nature of the emergency. It was about ten or fifteen minutes later that one of the doctors decided to conduct some tests and asked me to leave the room for a while.

"The diagnosis, of course, was very disheartening, and by the time I next saw PB he had gone into a coma."

Paul and I promptly set out for the Bon Samaritain Hospital which was only a fifteen-minute walk away.

The hospital staff were all extremely kind. The nurse explained to me that she felt my father had been hanging on in the coma by sheer willpower until my arrival. She took his hand and said into his ear, "Mr Brunton, your son has arrived, your son has arrived from America!"

The doctor told me that PB had suffered a massive cerebral hemorrhage and his condition was very serious indeed. They did not know whether or not he would ever emerge from the coma and told me, "Even if he recovers he will be paralyzed, but to what extent we can't tell."

Paul returned to the apartment while I settled down to wait for what could be an indeterminate time. After a while the nurses went off for their tea break and I was left alone with my father. I took him by the hand and told him, "It's all right, PB, I'm here, Kenneth is here." His eyes opened and his consciousness fluttered back fully, but he was unable to speak. Yet I definitely detected recognition in his eyes. After about ten minutes the nurses returned and he closed his eyes again.

I asked whether we could have a larger room as I intended to stay with him for whatever time it took. They then moved us to a larger room with an armchair next to the bed. Here I waited, and waited.

The evening dinner hour arrived and the nurses inquired whether I wanted to go downstairs to their small cafeteria. I said that I preferred to stay with my father and that in any case I was a vegetarian. So they very kindly brought me some cooked vegetables on a plate with some bread and I had the meal alongside PB's bed. The evening grew on and the nurses changed their shift. I continued to wait. But, I wonder to myself, what will happen? Supposing PB stays in his coma for days, for weeks, for months? What should I do? I have responsibilities back in the States. But I need not have been concerned; my father was a perfect gentleman in every way, and he was most considerate even to his transition.

At one o'clock in the morning I suddenly heard what I realized was a death rattle emerging from my father's throat. I was frightened. I had never heard one before. And in fact it turned out to be a series of death rattles as the body endeavored to expel the air from its frame. He emitted terrible sighs as though bemoaning all the ignorance in the world.

I rushed over to the bed and took my father in my arms. Suddenly his eyes opened and I felt the full consciousness of his powerful personality as they latched onto mine. I felt his *will* as though he loved me deeply and wanted to see his last fill of me. I received a series of mental messages, as clearly as if he were enunciating them out loud.

"What are you so upset about? We've gone through this dozens of times!" I heard inwardly as my tears fell upon his face.

The last message was, "We shall certainly meet again!"

Suddenly the room was illuminated with a white light and I felt tremendous forces present. It was as though I could almost hear the rustle of the angels' wings as they came to carry off my father. Whatever fear of death I might have had up to that time disappeared instantly; I know now that it is a beautiful transition for those of spiritual advancement. And my father was certainly such a one.

His eyes clouded and I felt that he had gone.

I kissed him and felt his head—it was deathly cold. Then, an illusion as I gazed into his eyes, it was as though he were laughing and saying, "Don't take it so seriously!" His visage was very smooth and peaceful.

After a while I went out and called the nurse. She came in and said, "He must have been a very good man, he has such a lovely face."

I said good night and went outside and walked back along the cobblestoned lanes to my father's apartment. I looked up and searched the sky for Orion's belt and then located the beautiful brilliant star of Sirius--my father's favorite to which he felt a strong affinity. I am reminded of his statement repeated in Volume 8 of his *Notebooks*: "When after the act of dying I shall be carried away to my own star, to Sothis of the Egyptians, Sirius of the westerners, I shall at last be happy." And I remember that Sirius also stands for the hidden teaching of hidden truth.

As I gazed, a shooting star flashed across my vision. "There goes PB," I thought.

* * * * *

As I lay in PB's bed for the remainder of that sleepless night I knew that I would seek retirement as soon as I could arrange my business affairs and devote the rest of my life to carrying out PB's work. I realized that I had been left behind in this lifetime so that I could take care of his personal and business affairs and he knew that I was both discreet enough and competent to handle them.

So the next morning I went to see his lawyer and the cremation society and made the arrangements for his body to be removed from the hospital and prepared for cremation three days later. There were a lot of details to be taken care of, but somehow I managed.

There was a gentle rain all day and I recalled the French Catholic saying: "God pours out his benediction when a good soul passes." And July 31, 1981 witnessed both a solar eclipse and a new moon.

On Thursday morning Paul Cash and I went to the church

of St Martin in Vevey for the cremation. The undertaker asked me if I wanted one last look at my father, and I said no. I knew that what remained of his body was not the real PB. So the body was cremated and we had a few minutes of silence.

I then had to arrange with the American consul in Geneva for a mortuary certificate, along with the hospital's death certificate, and a permit from the Cantonal police to allow the remains to be encased in a container with a transit permit to allow me to take them to New York. Everyone was most cooperative. Patsy G. Stephens, the consul, provided me with the appropriate documents.

By the end of the week everything was in place and I was ready to leave. Paul Cash agreed to stay on and arrange for shipping the furniture from my father's apartment which I decided to give to the Wisdom's Goldenrod Center for Philosophic Studies, along with his *objets d'art* and I asked Paul to distribute these to those students who had been chiefly helpful in working on his *Notebooks*.

And so on August 1, 1988, I took the 11:03 A.M. train from Vevey to Geneva firmly clasping the ashes of my father in a large sealed metal container. In Geneva I went straight to the apartment of one of the many people whom I had telephoned that week to announce the news of my father's death. This was Dr Stefan de Somogyi-Schill, a longtime friend of my father's. In fact back in 1947 my father had arranged a meeting for me with Dr de Schill, who was a member of the Hungarian aristocracy, in the hope that it might show me what good manners were, and I was indeed duly impressed by his charm and politeness. We did not keep in touch and I had not seen him for thirty-four years. But when the taxi dropped me at his apartment in Geneva suddenly the events of the past week flooded in on me and became overpowering. I had held up while I had duties to perform but now the reaction set in. Stefan adroitly noticed my condition, being a skilled psychologist, so he excused himself on the grounds that he had work to do before we could go to lunch, and set me down at a table with a full bottle of Johnny Walker scotch, a glass and ice. Although I am not a drinking man, I finished half that bottle by the time he returned.

After lunch I took a taxi to the airport and caught my plane to New York. I remember I was seated next to a Czech woman tennis player on her way to compete in the US Open at Forest Hills. Normally, being a tennis fan, I would have engaged her in conversation but this time I kept quiet holding tightly on to my metal container of PB's ashes. I did not let go of it and took it with me even to the bathroom. I found myself talking to it: "It's alright, PB, we're going home."

Upon my return to my office I sent out a letter to all the names in his address books announcing his transition. The short note ended with, "The outer PB has gone, but the inner PB lives on in the hearts of all who love him." I received many replies and people wrote how much he had meant in their lives.

I then asked our mutual friend, the Italian sculptor, Erna Rosa King, who had been a student of PB for many years if she would design an urn in the shape of a book to contain his ashes. She quickly created a striking container on which she engraved a quote I had chosen from page 189 of *The Wisdom of the Overself*:

> We shall certainly survive the sharp sting of the
> scorpion of death

It seemed entirely appropriate for I know now that PB continues more than ever as I feel him working through me and indeed I feel myself taking on his habits, his work patterns. Yes, we are closer now than in life because now our relationship is from the inside out, rather than the outside in. I feel his inspiration daily. As situations arise I find myself asking what would PB do in this situation, "What would he say?" And always I try to live up to him to make him proud of me.

Later I composed the following short notice which subsequently was included in reprintings of his books worldwide:

A PERSONAL NOTE

Paul Brunton died July 27, 1981, in Vevey, Switzerland. Born in London in 1898, he authored eleven books from *A Search in Secret India* published in 1934 to *The Spiritual Crisis of Man* in 1952. Dr Brunton is generally recognized as having helped introduce yoga and meditation to the West, and for presenting their philosophical background in nontechnical language.

His mode of writing was to jot down paragraphs as inspiration occurred. Often these were penned on the backs of envelopes or along margins of newspapers as he strolled amid the flower gardens bordering Lake Geneva. They later were typed and classified by subject. He then would edit and meld these paragraphs into a coherent narrative.

Paul Brunton lived in Switzerland for the last twenty years of his life. He liked the mild climate and majestic mountain scenery. Visitors and correspondence came from all over the world. He played an important role in the lives of many.

"PB," as he is known to many readers, was a gentle man. An aura of kindliness emanated from him. His scholarly learning was forged in the crucible of life. His spirituality shone forth like a beacon. But he discouraged attempts to form a cult around him: "You must find your own PB within yourselves," he used to say.

CHAPTER 27

The Notebooks

My father had not published a new book since *The Spiritual Crisis of Man* in 1952. When I asked him why he replied, "Oh, you know how it is. You're a publisher: the moment you tell your publisher you're working on a new book he gives you no peace; he wants to know when will the manuscript be ready, and he hounds you—and I don't like being under that sort of pressure!"

Yet he kept writing daily. His method was to jot down ideas related to the spiritual quest as they arose in the unbroken stillness of his mind. He often jotted down thoughts on the backs of envelopes or the corners of newspapers as he strolled amid the flower gardens of Montreux which were his favorite. He even kept a pad and pencil by his bedside. These notes he subsequently categorized according to twenty-eight primary subjects or "categories" ranging from readily accessible advice on emotions and ethics to the most abstruse notions of philosophy. He had twenty-eight folders and he would drop each note into the appropriate folder. When there were enough notes in a folder, they would be sent off for typing. Many of these were typed over the years by his longterm student Loraine Stevens, who served him faithfully.

Once back from being typed, the notes were reviewed and usually revised into a more literary form, typed again to include the revisions, and then filed again according to their appropriate category. Most of these were eventually reviewed a second time, polished still further, typed again and filed in a notebook as completed. These were the three stages of the "Ideas" series in my father's notebooks, which he called "Rough Ideas," "Middle Ideas," and simply "Ideas," respectively.

The files grew steadily. But although he sometimes talked about the possibility of publishing a new book, he never did.

Several times through the years, he said to me: "When I've gone, you must decide what should be published." But we both knew the material would need a great deal of sorting and arranging and retyping in addition to the normal copy-editing process—and it would be a tremendous undertaking. Early on I had imagined that I would retire and tackle it myself with the help of one or two friends. But it was to be larger than that.

During his 1977 visit to Wisdom's Goldenrod Center for Philosophic Studies, my father decided to accept Anthony Damiani's offer of editorial assistance by his own students. Consequently PB decided to allow a few of them to spend time with him in Switzerland so he could train them accordingly. He chose three young men, all of whom had studied his philosophy extensively under Anthony. They were Paul Randall Cash, Timothy J. Smith and Edward McKeon. Each of these individuals spent several months with PB. Several students from Wisdom's Goldenrod were also able to make extended visits with him in his last few years. Each of these people helped PB with a variety of mundane chores and cooking in his last few years, and each participated to some extent with helping him keep up with correspondence and reorganize his literary materials.

Interestingly, none of the three people PB eventually selected to prepare his notebooks for publication after he was gone knew of that intention during the time they spent with him. Each had his own unique experience of PB, which involved much more than simply getting acquainted with PB's methods for handling literary material. By that time PB was a thoroughly practiced master of seeing what a student most urgently needed to learn by way of balance and self-integration and adjusting his own side of the relationship so as to accommodate those needs. So the method of "training" varied with each individual. Perhaps some day, if there is sufficient interest, an account of their experiences of this process will be published. But for now, on with the progress of the notebooks project itself.

Paul Randall Cash, called "Randy" by many of his friends, was the last of these students to work with PB. He was with PB at the time of his fatal stroke in July 1981, and promptly telephoned me as I have related in another chapter. During the days that followed in Switzerland, I informed Randy of PB's plans for posthumous publication of his notebooks, and Randy related the unexpected and somewhat overwhelming news to Ed and Tim. During the time each of them had spent with him, they had become well aware of how large a task preparing the notebooks for publication would be. I brought back my father's personal papers and Randy stayed on in Switzerland to handle the packing and shipping of the notebooks and other materials (and indeed of my father's furniture), and disposing of various details involved in clearing my father's apartment. During the next few weeks, Randy had able assistance from another of PB's close students, Mrs Claire Pierpoint, and from a young Lebanese man who had first spotted PB on a street in Lausanne only a few months before and intuitively recognized that here was a truly remarkable man. We have since lost touch with this young man, but if he should by chance read this account, I would welcome the opportunity of thanking him.

When the notebooks arrived in the United States they were in no condition for publication. More than seventy notebooks were crowded with pages of single-spaced type on thin paper. There were more than 17,000 pages altogether, including original work, research notes, and comments on writings of others. The most important section was the section, containing more than 7,000 pages, of the various stages involved in the "Ideas" notebooks.

Then in September of 1981 began a lengthy and painstaking labor of love. Most of the original pages were of very thin paper that had been used to conserve shelf space, and few of them left any room for the needed editorial work. Further, no one involved in the project felt that these original pages should be marked in any way. So the first step was to make three photocopies of the entire notebooks: one as a reading copy for the Wisdom's Goldenrod library, one for editorial work, and a third as a vault copy for reference in the event of any pages' being lost and to minimize the need to handle the original notebooks. Wisdom's Goldenrod rented a quality photocopying machine which was then operated almost continuously for a month by volunteers from the group. Then Randy and Tim and Ed started reading the "Ideas" section and meeting to discuss how to approach their part of the job. Meanwhile, the library of Wisdom's Goldenrod became a very popular place, with a regular turnover of students reading sections of the library copy nearly all hours of the day and night.

Anthony Damiani coordinated this process and spent virtually every free minute of his own time reading in the notebooks. Within a few weeks he declared that these notes were by far the most significant achievement he had ever seen— and we all knew that he had extensively studied practically everything available in English in this field! He said that had this material been available to him in his youth, he could have saved at least twenty years of study and avoided dozens of mistakes he had made through having to learn by the harder way of his own trial and error. He also said that he knew in the beginning that there was some reason guiding him to found Wisdom's Goldenrod, though until now he hadn't known what that reason was. Now he knew: guaranteeing that these notes reach the public in the best possible form.

His enthusiasm and commitment to readying the notebooks for publication in the shortest amount of time ignited his students, and all helped in some way to move things forward. For personal reasons, Ed McKeon was unable to take a full third of the editorial responsibility and was forced to limit his participation to helping with less demanding aspects of the work as his circumstances allowed. Eventually, Anthony, Tim, and Randy had assembled an organized volunteer staff with a variety of skills and provided enough training in specific aspects of the task to start seeing orderly progress. What is most remarkable about the description that follows is that nearly all of the individuals involved held their regular full or part time jobs throughout the process, many of them are parents with families to care for and support, and all did their work on evenings or weekends or whenever else time was available.

While this work was in its formative stages a "cataloging group" was formed to check all three sets of the photocopies against each other and the original notebooks to ensure complete correspondence of the copies and the originals. This group also produced a complete breakdown of the overall contents of the notebooks.

The biggest complication that had to be dealt with in the early stages, requiring the greatest investment of time, was that PB had improved the ordering and naming of his twenty-eight "Ideas" categories at least three times through the years. So even though the Ideas material all bore numbers indicating category 1 or 10 or 28 as the case may be, those numbers often did not correspond to the same meanings. Randy and Tim first assigned a general number of 1–28 to each of the many thousands of individual Ideas entries (many of which were only a line or two in length!), bringing them more closely into alignment with PB's latest version—the one he had told them gave the order in which the material should be presented. But these twenty-eight general groupings each still included much too much material to allow for going immediately to copy-editing and sequencing for publication. Breaking each group down further into more differentiated subthemes had to be done before they could tell how much of the material was repetitive and how much of it introduced genuinely new ideas or valuable subtleties. Two major developments then came into place to expedite this next step.

First, to track and expedite the unavoidable shuffling of hundreds of thousands of individual items, it was proposed that the entire Ideas series be converted to an electronic format. This proposal offered many advantages: a sufficiently sophisticated computer database would not only accelerate the process of manipulating the material through its many subcategories, it would also enforce the orderliness of a process that could easily become unmanageable; further, having all the material in an electronic format could save tens of thousands of dollars in typesetting costs when the notes were finally ready for publication.

Once the editors had been sold on this idea, a highly qualified group of computer people developed the software and acquired the hardware needed for such an unprecedented undertaking. This group soon worked out a remarkably sophisticated system groomed specifically to the needs presented to them by Randy and Tim. It would be difficult to assign a financial value to the hundreds of hours these people put in—on an entirely volunteer basis—to adapt their high-tech skills to the project's needs.

Simultaneously, other Wisdom's Goldenrod volunteers went to work on putting the notes themselves through an equally sophisticated process. First, dozens of volunteers spent hundreds of hours at computer keyboards. They were given pages from the working photocopy of the notebooks as soon as Randy and Tim had assigned category numbers, and then they typed each entry, along with an appropriate code identifying the original notebook number and the new category, into the database.

As the entry of each notebook into the database was completed, a new printout of the entire notebook was generated from the database, which was then proofread against the original working photocopy by another group of volunteers. Once this group had done its work and the needed changes were entered into the database, the database contained a very reliable electronic copy of the "Ideas," organized into the latest version of the 1–28, and also able to be recalled by its original notebook number as well.

New printouts were then produced, organized this time into the new categories Randy and Tim had assigned. This printout went to another group of volunteers who would break each category down into more refined subthemes. While the other parts of the process were going on, Randy and Tim had familiarized a few people with the various subthemes appropriate to given categories, explaining how they would like the process of "sub-classing" to be done. Those people in turn took the responsibility of training and supervising others to help with this "refining" process. As various people developed a reasonable amount of expertise in this process, a group of "class captains" emerged.

Each of the twenty-eight categories eventually had a class captain who developed an outline of major subthemes in his or her chosen category. The printout was then literally cut up into thousands of pieces, with each piece containing one individual "para." A staff of people working under the captain sorted these individual pieces into a "cut-and-paste" version of the category. Each person involved at this stage organized a selected section of these small pieces of paper into an orderly arrangement, by theme, that identified even the tiniest of sub-sub-themes of a given idea. They then arranged these pages in an order that "ranked" the paras as "yes," "no," or "maybe" for publication. The captain tracked and supervised each person's work within his or her category and then presented a completed "cut-and-paste" of the category to individuals working closely with Tim and Randy. These individuals would then make whatever changes they felt were necessary before passing this completed cut-and-paste along to Randy and Tim, who were then able to select the material they wanted to use for publication.

At this stage Randy and Tim assigned codes indicating class, subclass, and sub-subclass to every item in the cut-and-paste, as well as codes indicating whether or not the given item would be published or set aside. Because they were in regular contact with one another, they could also decide at this stage if something should be moved from one major class to another, and thus maintain an overview of the classing and selection process as a whole.

The next stage involved careful computer work, feeding Randy and Tim's more detailed codes for individual paras back into the database. This work was done, with remarkable speed and accuracy, by another small group of dedicated volunteers.

Then the more refined database could provide a printout of the paras selected selected for publication. The computer generated these paras in thematic groupings, but the order of paras within a given grouping was random. Copies of this printout were used for two purposes. One was distributed to a group of volunteer copy-editors. While this group performed light but careful copyediting, Randy and Tim each did a final reading of their respective categories. In the course of this reading, they determined the chapter structure and substructure for publication, eliminated an additional 10–15% of the paras, and did a small amount of deliberate arranging within themes to enhance readability of the finished product. The copy-edited and selected material then went to Randy for a final check before all the results of this stage of the process were fed into the computer and double-checked for accurate entry.

The completely edited result was incorporated into a final printout, which was sent along with an electronic copy for typesetting. When typeset galleys returned from the typesetter, a faithful staff of volunteer proofreaders inevitably found a few more errors to fix, and did so.

Simultaneously with the checking of the galleys, various individuals worked on making an index for each category.

The final step was making the typeset galleys, with corrections, into facing pages suitable for use as camera copy by the printer.

Every stage of progress in each department was carefully tracked, recorded, and reported regularly to Randy and Tim by a small tracking group.

This entire process was done on a volunteer basis and involved nearly everyone at Wisdom's Goldenrod. Though there was a regular turnover within staffs through the seven years the project took, there were always at least a dozen people working regularly.

But while this editorial process took shape, a big question mark remained concerning how I should handle actual publication of the Notebooks. The training my father had given Tim and Randy called for a remarkably systematic approach to how the materials should be presented. Given the sheer number of pages involved, publishing the notebooks according to his guidelines would inevitably involve a great deal of time and a very large financial risk for their publisher. PB had so effectively withdrawn himself from public life that sales of his earlier books had diminished to a mere trickle, making that risk understandably unattractive to most publishers. While a number of them were quite willing to experiment with publishing limited selections from the notebooks with the hope of eventually being able to accommodate the approach his young editors had been trained to complete, none dared to commit to the full series as PB had conceived it.

This situation was something of a dilemma for me for a while, as PB had left me in charge of choosing publishers for his writings. On one side were PB's young editors confirming my own feelings that the late writings should be published in the form PB wanted; on the other side was my own much more extensive knowledge of the current realities of the publishing world, telling me that some sort of compromise was all but inevitable. But the enthusiasm and dedication of the Goldenrod group as a whole was remarkable: maybe something unusual was in fact in the process of happening.

At this stage, a decision made by Swedish publisher Robert Larson became a key factor in the way the situation ultimately resolved itself. A few words about Robert are appropriate by way of background to what came to pass.

In the 1970s, Robert's Swedish company began to publish Anna Prim Bornstein's Swedish translations of PB's early books. Robert's relationship with Anna led eventually to a series of meetings with PB, meetings which inspired Robert to dedicate a large part of his energies to practicing the spiritual quest himself and being as helpful as possible in making the ideas associated with it more readily available in Sweden. Anna also introduced Robert to Anthony Damiani, with whom she had studied herself for several years.

During the time of PB's transition (July 1981), Robert and his family and a number of PB's students from Sweden were visiting Wisdom's Goldenrod. When Robert learned later in that week of PB's notebooks, he told Anthony Damiani that he would help, in whatever way could be possible, to get the notebooks out in the form PB had set up. He said that even if it meant simply giving money, he would do that; but he also had the hope of doing more.

Robert had wanted for several years to open an American branch of his Swedish company. On the outside chance of possibly publishing the notebooks, he felt that the time had arrived for him to make that move. Anthony, convinced even then that a way would develop to bring the notebooks out according to PB's guidelines, encouraged him to do so, though he made it clear to Robert that at that time (August 1981) there seemed little chance of the notebooks' being available for publication by Robert's American subsidiary.

Robert talked subsequently with several of Anthony's students, including Tim Smith, Andrew Holmes and Randy

Cash. By April of 1982, Randy was working as director of the new company—dividing his time between putting together and editing a small list of initial titles, exploring market channels, and doing his share of the editorial work on the notebooks project.

Letters from readers throughout the world who had heard of the notebooks began to come to me. Even though Tim and Randy told me that they were years from being ready to publish the notebooks, I felt strongly that these letters meant something should come out sooner. After a series of discussions with Anthony, Tim, Randy, and a number of publishers, I succeeded in accommodating those requests. Anthony undertook the responsibility of pulling together a good selection of essays and essay fragments requiring little work to publish, and Randy and Tim took responsibility for putting together a "highlights" volume from the "Ideas" section of the notebooks—to give readers a sampling of what was to come. I selected from among the essays Anthony provided those in which Rider and Company (PB's British publishers) were most interested and then edited them lightly for publication in paperback by Rider in England and Samuel Weiser Inc. in the United States. Meanwhile Randy and Tim worked with Anthony and several volunteers on the book we initially decided to call *Perspectives on the Notebooks of Paul Brunton*. This volume affords a broad picture of the series as a whole, giving a representative selection of paragraphs for each of the twenty-eight categories.

My father's earlier books at this time were all available in paperback from Samuel Weiser Inc., whose president Donald Weiser steadfastly kept them in print even when their sales did not warrant it from a commercial viewpoint. But Weiser published only in paperback, and it obviously was necessary to have the *Notebooks* series proper appear first in cloth covers to obtain the serious review attention it deserved. So, reviewing our options and possibilities, I decided to accept Robert

Larson's request to publish the hardcover edition of *Perspectives* with Robert's new and untested company, Larson Publications Inc.

Perspectives was published in July, 1984, followed a few weeks later by the Rider edition of *Essays on the Quest* in August.

But by the summer of 1985 various difficulties were besetting the flow of the editorial project and Larson Publications was finding itself forced to revise its initial game plan. Robert had hoped to be able to support the growth of his American subsidiary by combining profits from the Swedish parent company with US sales of books with reasonably good commercial potential here. But a change in Swedish law concerning study circles, a drastic drop in the value of the Swedish kroner against the dollar, and slower American sales than he had hoped for combined to force some serious rethinking.

Robert and Randy agreed that getting PB's notebooks published as soon as possible should be their priority, and that grappling for more of a commercial foothold in the competitive US marketplace would simply take too much time from the process of readying the notebooks for publication. They met in July of 1985 and discussed options for how the notebooks publication project could be accelerated.

Until this time I had not been directly involved in the *Notebooks* publication project. I had been planning and implementing the vow I had made that sleepless night of my father's death when I had returned to his apartment and laid down in his bed. I knew then that I would leave the world of commercial publishing and devote myself to spreading my father's teaching to a wider, less sophisticated audience through writings and lectures. The words of my father, "I thought you were going to write in your retirement," echoed in my ears. But it took a couple of years to be able to disengage myself from my business responsibilities and obligations before I could officially retire in 1983. Even then I found myself in demand as a freelance publishing consultant from my erstwhile competitors and other companies. And this acted as a sort of decompression chamber after many years of high-powered schedules.

When I heard about the problems confronting the publishers of the *Notebooks*, my first reaction was to offer both my professional services and financing in a cooperative commercial venture. Within a few days, however, I woke up with the complete solution clearly outlined in my mind. I needed to establish a foundation to take over all the publishing activities of my father's works and to remove them thereby from the commercial vibration. Further, a foundation would provide an ongoing vehicle to perpetuate my father's works and teachings independently of what may or may not be profitable in any particular year. It could make possible a number of options that simply would not be viable or as purely motivated in a commercial context.

Within a matter of days, we formed a working board of directors from those engaged in various aspects of the *Notebooks* project and initiated the process of applying for non-profit, tax-exempt status for the Paul Brunton Philosophic Foundation. Shortly thereafter, I invited a number of outside personages to serve on an advisory council for the new foundation. These included Dr Elisabeth Kubler-Ross; Srimata Gayatri Devi of the Vedanta Ashrama; Dr Elizabeth Fenske, President of Spiritual Frontiers Fellowship; Dr Kenneth Ring, President of the International Association for Near-Death Studies; Rev Paul V. Johnson, President, Spiritual Advisory Council; Donald Weiser, longtime publisher of PB's works in paperback; Mrs Barbara Bunce of the Christian Fellowship Society of Great Britain; Dr Arthur Broekuysen, longtime student of PB; Judge Robert D. Ericsson of Chicago; Mrs Gilda Frantz of Los Angeles, a leading Jungian psychotherapist; Donald Keys, Director of Planetary Citizens; and Barbara Somerfield, President of Aurora Press. These advisory councilors have helped promote *The Notebooks* through their own organizations and I am grateful to them for the publicity they have given in their newsletters and journals spreading the word to their members.

Work went on apace, and the foundation was soon efficiently performing the activities it had been conceived for. But because of the complexities of working out all the legal requirements in the best possible way for what we intend to accomplish, more than a year passed before all the needed documentation was firmly in place. The Paul Brunton Philosophic Foundation was duly incorporated under the laws of New York State as a cultural foundation early in 1987, and later received tax-exempt status from the Internal Revenue Service under Section 501 (c) (3) of the Internal Revenue Code, being classified as an organization under Section 170 (b) (1) (a) (vi).

I had previously waived royalties from *The Notebooks* and subsequently turned over the copyrights to the foundation.

PB used to say that if an idea is right it unfolds smoothly and quickly. Such was the case with the Paul Brunton Philosophic Foundation. It fell into place remarkably. The legal description of the foundation is "an international cultural and educational organization, a non-sectarian foundation to further the aims of philosophy as demonstrated in the writings and personal teachings of Paul Brunton. Its activities include but are not limited to the publication and international dissemination of the philosophic ideas of Paul Brunton and other individuals whose work is in alignment with the overall purpose of the foundation."

Once the foundation took responsibility for publication of *The Notebooks*, the remaining fifteen volumes of the sixteen-volume series were issued at regular intervals through 1988. The foundation has published them in both cloth and paperback editions. Whereas the former are mainly intended for libraries and serious PB students, the latter are aimed at the general market and their covers have attractive colorful illustrations to catch the eye of the passerby. On the back covers of the paperback editions are different photographs of PB taken through the years.

Initial reception to the series has been very favorable. Some of the early reviews included:

"Vigorous, clear-minded, and independent . . . "—*Library Journal* (on *Perspectives*)

". . . the work as a whole is a rich vein of wisdom to be mined by the interested and the spiritually concerned."—*Library Journal* (on Volume 4)

". . . sensible and compelling. His work can stand beside that of such East-West bridges as Merton, Suzuki, Huxley, Watts, and Radhakrishnan."—*Choice*

"A simple, straightforward guide to how philosophical insights of East and West can help to create beauty, joy, and meaning in our lives."—*East West Journal*

"Attuned to today's holistic health movement. Healing of the self is the guiding principle behind these writings."—*Publishers Weekly*

Altogether to date, the series has received a large number of reviews any publisher would be proud of. A listing of excerpts from those reviews is available in a brochure from the foundation.

As of this writing (early 1989) the first volume, *Perspectives*, has been reprinted twice. Volumes 2, 3, 4, 5, 6, 7, 9, and 11 have been reprinted once each, and volumes 10, 12, 13, and 14 will probably have to be reprinted by the time this book is available. Volumes that have been especially popular include *Perspectives*, Volume 2 (*The Quest*), Volume 4 (*Meditation*), Volume 11 (*The Sensitives: Dynamics and Dangers of Mysticism*), Volume 13 (*Relativity, Philosophy, and Mind*), and Volume 14 (*Inspiration and the Overself*).

CHAPTER 28

My Impressions from India

In 1960 when the State Department asked me to go to Burma as a publishing consultant, as mentioned previously, they also suggested that I go via India and stop off in Bombay, Madras and Calcutta to see their book operations which came under the United States Information Agency. I welcomed the opportunity and was thrilled to see my first eastern sunrise in Karachi where I had to change planes. Later when we landed at Bombay's Juhu airport and I took the airline bus downtown, I was overwhelmed by the fantastic variety of colors— this was indeed another world. My heart went out to the crowds huddled on the sidewalks and I felt an overwhelming pity for them and vowed I would come back and help them. And I did—within a year I was back living in India with a mandate to form a publishing company. But that's another story.

My next stop was Madras in southern India, where I was met at the airport by an Embassy driver who took me to my hotel. It happened to be December 31 and the driver informed me that the next day, New Year's Day, was a holiday for him and would I like him to show me some of the sights? I gladly accepted and after spending my first night under a mosquito net at the Connemara Hotel and listening to the raucous revelry coming from the bar downstairs I was glad to be picked up and taken out by the driver next morning. He showed me the Deer Park, the Monkey Bridge and other sights. Suddenly the driver said to me, "You know, sir, you remind me of an English gentleman who used to come into town once a week during the war and would hire my taxi, as I was a taxi driver then, to take him around for the day on his errands." Suddenly I realized he was talking about my father!

More than twenty years later, almost fifty years after the publication of *A Search in Secret India* and not long after PB's death, I was again in India. I retraced my father's steps and journeyed around the country to give "in memoriam" lectures in his honor. I learned that his name is still held there in highest esteem. Many Indians told me that they discovered their own country's spiritual dimension from this very book. I made a pilgrimage to the same ashram he discovered and offered my obeisance in the meditation hall where Ramana Maharshi had lived. I saw the small bungalow my father had inhabited, and I gazed up at towering Arunachala.

The highlight of my trip was my encounter with His Holiness Sri Shankara Acharya, the Spiritual Head of South India, whom my father describes in Chapter VIII of *A Search in Secret India*. I had no prior intention of meeting him, but upon leaving the Ramanashram decided to seek him out. After I had driven along country roads for three hours before reaching the village where he was staying, history seemed to repeat itself. I was first told there was no chance of my being granted an audience with him. However a friendly disciple agreed to submit my card and returned with the news that His Holiness would receive me at the rear of the temple to avoid the crowds milling in front. His slight figure, clad in a saffron robe, reflected his ninety-one years. I told him I was the son of Paul Brunton. He replied briefly. The interpreter informed me, "He knows!" His Holiness spoke again. "He has been waiting for you! He has been expecting you," said the interpreter. But how did he even know of me? How did he know I was in India, I wondered to myself? I held out a copy of the book and showed him his photograph, taken when he was thirty-eight. "I know!" was his comment.

At this point I had hoped to elicit his views on the world situation as had my father previously. But suddenly all questions melted as I felt an onrush of peace and love. All I could do was to prostrate myself in the time-honored tradition at the feet of His Holiness as he gave me his blessing. He then put around my neck a sacred *mala*, a garland fashioned from fragrant sandalwood. I wear it daily.

Thus the wheel came full circle half a century later.

CHAPTER 29

An Adept in Angkor Wat

Many PB readers have asked whether I can throw any light on the adept my father met at Angkor Wat. Yes, I can; but first let's reread the reference in question as published on page 43 of Volume 8 in the *Notebooks*.

> Although I was already travelling the road to the self-discovery of these truths, it is true that an apparently fortuitous meeting with an extraordinary individual at Angkor saved me from some of the time and labour involved in this process. For he turned out to be an adept in the higher philosophy who had not only had a most unusual personal history but also a most unusual comprehension of the problems which were troubling me. He put me through strange initiatory experiences in a deserted temple and then, with a few brief explanations of the hidden teachings, placed the key to their solutions in my hands. But after all it was only a key to the doorchamber itself, and not the entire treasure. These I had to ferret out for myself. That is to say, I was given the principle but had to work out the details, develop the applications, and trace out the ramifications for myself. I was provided with a foundation but had to erect the superstructure by my own efforts. And all this has been a task for so many years, a task upon which I am still engaged.

Next let me share with you a letter from PB to Myron Frantz written February 15, 1939, from the Siam-Indochina border:

My dear Myron and Nancy,

How do you do! I am still on the journey to India but unfortunately travelling backwards again! Have been asked by one of my spiritual superiors to proceed to Angkor, in French Indochina for certain purposes. There are immense old ruins there, surrounded by jungle. I must tell you that it was formerly the centre of our spiritual Adept-hierarchy, after they shifted from India; from Angkor they moved, hundreds of years later to Tibet, and now their departure from the latter land is imminent. Where will they go to next? This year, 1939, is highly critical from a spiritual standpoint, as a new momentum and impetus must be released into the world to save the TRUTH and give it to those who can take it in. The gods are watching the situation, we are not far from the turning point and it must be done this year. My return to the Orient was not too soon, and there is so much work to do that I have been continuously busy till far into the night since I last wrote you. Much coming and going, too, conferences, notes, etc., that I can do very little correspondence, but I wanted to send you a few more words.

The Supreme Priest of Siamese Buddhism has presented me with a tremendously heavy statue of Buddha, very old, which I shall bring back to the States eventually. I also received several gifts from the Chinese adepts, rare paintings which are highly magnetised.

At a midnight conference out in the jungle where was present one of the adepts who was adviser to the late Dalai Lama of Tibet for many years, we went through several rites and ceremonies in one of which I sent out special grace to the students in the West, including you.

Affectionately,
Paul

The reader is also directed to pages 197–202 in Volume 10 of the *Notebooks* for PB's account of his meetings in Angkor and the Secret Doctrine of the Khmers.

CHAPTER 30

Dreams

Following my father's death in July 1981 I entered a period of blankness, of mourning, of grief. My life had undergone a radical change and I felt abandoned, like a ship without a rudder.

But after two years as time assuaged the pain an interesting development occurred: I was to experience many vivid dreams of my father over a period of a further two years. These were dreams with a capital D. I would awaken from them suddenly with the sharp recollection of my father vividly imprinted upon my consciousness. I will override my normal desire for privacy concerning such matters to share some of them because they are indeed meaningful and a powerful testimony to the survival of consciousness after death.

Dream 1. I am walking alongside my father. I am saying, "Oh, I wish you were alive, there are so many interesting things going on in my life right now I would like to tell you about." Then my father turns to me and smiles, a beautiful smile, and I exclaim, "But you *are* alive!"

Dream 2. I am in line at the teller's cage of a bank. I note that the people around me are speaking French. In my arms I am holding several bags full of money. In front of me is a gentleman of slight build wearing a beret. When his turn comes for him to transact his business he takes off his beret and lays it on the counter. He finishes his transaction, turns, and walks to a spiral staircase which he starts descending, but he leaves his beret on the ledge at the teller's cage. I find myself torn between wanting to run after him with his beret and yet loath to put down the large bags of money which I hold in my arms. However I make the decision and put the money down at the teller's cage and run after him. I call out to him in French that he has forgotten his beret. He stops, turns and looks up at me with the most beautiful luminous smile—and I recognize my father!

Dream 3. My father and I are touring in an open convertible. I am at the wheel. I spot a French bakery and we stop to buy some bread. My father goes to the restroom and I wait for him in the car, eating from the loaf of bread. When my father returns he chides me for getting crumbs in the car. He tells me to wait until we can eat the bread properly outside the car.

Dream 4. My father and I enter an elegant restaurant crowded with beautiful people seated at tables with the finest linen, sparkling cutlery and cut crystal glassware. We are ushered to a table and we order tea and delicious French pastries.

Dream 5. I enter an Italian restaurant with some friends. We are ushered to a rear room. We sit down and examine the menu. Suddenly I exclaim, "PB was here! This is his handwriting on the menu!"

Dream 6. I am with PB in a foreign country but I do not know who he is. He says he has lost his key case and wishes to retrace his movements of the morning to try to find it. A woman declares she will not follow him, but I volunteer to do so. We cross a wide boulevard as the traffic is halted for a red light and in the middle of the street PB exclaims, "Here they are!" and bends over and picks up the case. We continue to cross the wide street. I observe PB closely. I see his features clearly. "What is my real relationship to him?" I wonder. We enter a small unpretentious cafe. The owner knows PB and in a foreign tongue directs us into the back, saying one word which obviously represents a dish which PB has enjoyed there before.

Dream 7. PB and I board a jet aircraft at the rear in Europe to travel to New York. PB goes to the front row and sits down. For some reason I do not follow him but I sit at the back of the aircraft. Then after a while I go to the front and find an empty seat beside PB and I sit in it. But after an announcement is made that the flight will be delayed, we disembark and I find we are in Rome airport. I leave PB as I go off to try to ascertain when the flight will take off. I find myself walking down a main street and come to a corner with other streets branching off it. I decide to have a coffee and some bread in a little shop and pay the woman in Italian lira. Then I notice that I have passed a woman who is carrying a bundle and she is crying piteously and looking at me accusingly. I feel sorry for her and go to give her some money.

Dream 8. I dreamed I was walking alongside my father and suddenly he broke into conversation seemingly at random as he often did. "My present teacher is Amenhotep," he said. "He lives in Florida where he grows a new kind of vegetation which emits health-giving properties. The inhabitants of the area report they feel a tremendous improvement in wellbeing as a result." As my father talked I saw the image of a large wheat field with the ears of golden wheat rippling in the gentle breeze. "Yes, Amenhotep is one of my best teachers," he said. I interjected, "Oh, my teacher is pretty good too!" looking meaningfully at him. Here the dream ended. It was very lifelike and realistic and my father's voice sounded exactly as it used to.

Next morning I looked up my father's two-volume type-script entitled "Egyptian Notes" to discover that Amenhotep IV was the original name of the Pharaoh Akhnaton, spouse of Queen Nefertiti. This was of particular significance to me. I had long felt an interest in this iconoclastic pharaoh who proclaimed the oneness of the Creator and the unity of Mind. I had admired his using the symbol of the sun to represent the Higher Power, and indeed had quoted his "Hymn to the Sun" in my own first book, *Live Life First Class!* It is one of the great inspired creations in the world of literature. I had had several discussions with my father about the Sun meditations which result in one developing a personal relationship with the sun—or rather *That* for which it stands. I believe it was the Theosophists, among others, who state that behind the physical sun is a spiritual sun, the heart of our universe. And Akhnaton declared 3,500 years ago: "The supreme creator of the universe is the One God to whom, through the light of the Sun, all eyes and hearts and minds must be directed."

So I was particularly pleased to find that my father's Egyptian notebooks spoke very highly of Akhnaton. My father believed him to be a spiritual sage and commented upon the large number of accomplishments he had achieved before his early death at twenty-eight. In fact, on page 83 in category 25 of the *Notebooks*, PB writes, "Include the name of Akhnaton as an illuminated mahatma when quoting Jesus, Buddha, etc., as examples." (See Volume 16, *Enlightened Mind, Divine Mind*.)

How did I interpret this dream? My physical health was far from perfect at this time and the harsh northern winters aggravated my heart disease and arthritic conditions. So I had been considering spending the winters in Florida to see if the warmer weather would ameliorate my physical problems. Therefore I took this dream to signify a message from my father that wintering in Florida would indeed help my health. (In the event this proved to be so and I felt twenty years younger as soon as I arrived in the sunny south from the cold north.) But why had he mentioned Akhnaton and especially using the original name of Amenhotep rather than the name by which he was generally known? That I cannot explain. Except that the Egyptians worshipped Sirius, the Dog Star, because its rising marks the annual flooding of the Nile irrigating the land and crops, and my father had written that his spiritual home was Sirius and that he would be carried there after his death! But I feel it quite possible that Amenhotep could still exist and still be connected to his Egyptian incarnation—or for all I know, he could have been an *avatar* like Krishna or Christ and still employ that particular individualistic vibration in a different sphere. In fact, my father had confided in me many years ago that as a young man he had traveled astrally with his first teacher, my godfather, Mr Thurston (after whom I was named). He said that Thurston had taken him to an astral university, but he had not given me any details. So it is possible that he could still be attending this astral university and studying under Akhnhaton. But this is sheer conjecture. (Yet . . . in his notes about Mr Thurston I have just found this cryptic sentence: "Amenhotep is connected with M and us." M here refers to "Brother M," the spiritual name of Mr Thurston!)

A few days later, browsing in a bookstore, I looked up the meaning of *wheat* in a book on dream interpretation and found it means "good health, a sense of well-being." How nicely it all fits together!

Next, for a non-dream, at least one that occurred in broad daylight. Just the other day while walking along Fifth Avenue in New York City and feeling the onrush of the harsh materialistic vibrations swirling around me, I sought relief by trying to go within to the secret place. Suddenly, to my amazement, I looked down and saw that I was wearing the short trousers that British schoolboys wear, together with my school woolen stockings, and I realized that I felt like a child of four or five years old—and my hand was firmly clasped in my father's! As we walked along all fear and trepidation left me and I felt a wonderful sense of confidence and protection emanating from him. What a marvelous experience! For the next few days I was able to recall this experience and feel the touch of his hand interlaced in my own.

And finally this too was not a dream—yet a distinct visitation from PB. I awoke with the vivid impression of my father having just kissed my cheek, so vivid that I could feel the scrape of the stubble of his beard. Even more, I was aware of his presence. Every pup knows its parents instinctively. There is no doubt in my mind that PB himself had visited me—and bestowed upon me this kiss of Grace, for which I am devoutly thankful.

Anyway, perhaps in the years since his passing I have been enabled to serve him and this remains my highest wish and desire. And as I look up into the night sky at the beautiful star Sirius there seems to be a wink of approval.

AFTERWORD

I wish to thank all those who urged me to write these reminiscences of my father. Although I was reluctant at first, nevertheless I realized that it was my duty and in fact I have enjoyed it. Many memories have been resurrected and revived. I have relived close moments with my father. I have felt his guiding hand help me with this project. The work has gone smoothly and effortlessly. It has been a sort of catharsis. I have enjoyed being once again through these pages with him who was dearer than life itself. And I look forward to going home soon to be reunited with him.

In this personalized account I have attempted to minimize repetition of any situations or comments which PB has made in any of his books—particularly in Volume 8 of his *Notebooks—Reflections on My Life and Writings*. So the reader is directed to read and reread that particular volume for a thorough understanding of my father's thoughts about life in general and his own in particular.

I realize that my narrative will disappoint many who had expected a chronological sequence of dates and facts. Why these seem important to them, I do not know—except that it is the traditional way to present a biography. But my father did not follow tradition. He thought far and struck out for himself. Perhaps it is because most people think in terms of time as a straight line and therefore would like to know about my father's life from his birth to his death in the proper order. But my father himself proved the illusoriness of time in *The Hidden Teaching Beyond Yoga*. It is not a straight line.

I have attempted to provide a study of my father as he was, the personality behind the public figure. For to me PB was always the same—whether as a young man in the reading rooms of London libraries or as a seeker after truth in India, or as the mature PB of the fifties and sixties, or as the elderly frailer figure of his later years. It is all PB, the one and only PB, to me. Therefore I have subtitled this book *A Personal View* for that is what it is and it pretends to be naught else. I offer it in the hope it will provide his thousands of readers with a glance at the man, the human being, behind the Paul Brunton whose books they read.

Writing this book has entailed reliving my life—which was inextricably intertwined with my father's. It has been an intensive experience.

Now it is all over, for the present anyway. PB and all of them I knew so dearly for so many years have gone before, and I am left behind.

> When I remember all
> The friends, so linked together,
> I've seen around me fall
> Like leaves in wintry weather,
> I feel like one
> Who treads alone
> Some banquet hall deserted,
> Whose lights are fled,
> Whose garlands dead,
> And all but he departed.
>
> Thomas Moore, 1779–1852

"I do not forget those who do not forget me," PB once said.

INDEX